Life's Journey Must Go On

Linda M. Sundve

WESTBOW
PRESS
A DIVISION OF THOMAS NELSON

WestBow Press books may be ordered through booksellers or by contacting:

WestBow Press
A Division of Thomas Nelson
1663 Liberty Drive
Bloomington, IN 47403
www.westbowpress.com
1-(866) 928-1240

ISBN: 978-1-4497-2553-2 (sc)
ISBN: 978-1-4497-2554-9 (hc)
ISBN: 978-1-4497-2552-5 (ebk)

Library of Congress Control Number: 2011914922

Printed in the United States of America

WestBow Press rev. date: 08/25/2011

In loving memory of my family
who brought happiness to my life.
During the short period I had with each of you,
you taught me much about life,
joy, adventure, laughter, sorrow,
how to love, and, most of all,
how to live and
appreciate every moment
that is given to me.

Special memory and love to my family Gary, Chad, Kirk,
Goldie, Louis, Doris, and Paul

From the Author

❧

This book tells a true story that was derived from one major event in 1977. Even though it has been over three decades, the memory of this event is still so vivid. Time has not faded the traumatic occurrence from my mind. Over the last year, God has awakened me in the middle of the night to remind me of events that need to be shared and has given me the strength to write about each one.

All Scriptures are taken from the Revised Standard Version, The New Oxford Annotate Bible with the Apocrypha, Copyright 1965, 1977 by Oxford University Press, Inc.

Forward

❧

Dear Readers:

Linda and I spent much of our growing-up years together. She lived near a neighborhood grocery store, and we would often meet there. We rode to church together, as I was usually picked up and delivered by her mom.

All three of us, Dan, Linda, and I, attended Northwest Nazarene College. When Dan and I married in 1966, Linda was my maid of honor. After she met Gary, the four of us spent much time together.

Dan and I lived in a two-bedroom house, and as "poor college students," we decided to let someone else have the extra bedroom. That person was Gary Sundve. The hours we spent together were delightful. I can still hear Gary's laugh after all these years.

Dan and Paul, Gary's brother, drove a school bus, and Gary was the mechanic for the bus company. These three were always doing something in or to cars. Dan bought a totaled 1964 Cadillac that had been hit at both ends. The three of them got that car in running order. Dan was able to drag race it (without our parents' knowledge for years). When the boys were on bus trips, Linda and I would do canning or anything that would stretch our meager budgets.

In June of 1968, Linda and Gary married and by August of 1969, we moved to Washington. They helped us load our belongings, and we traveled together to Sunnyside. Gary and Linda continued to take a school bus, which they were delivering to an Oregon bus company. Later, they moved to Oregon, but we always kept in contact.

Our last weekend with the Sundve family was Veterans Day weekend, November 1977. On our way to their house, we detoured to an emergency room, so we arrived much later than we had planned. It was the first time that all four of our children had been together. That weekend, we did lots of great things, including going to the Organ Grinder for pizza. I thank God so much for that weekend full of memories!

As soon as I heard about the wreck, and I was able to talk with Linda, her first words were "Didn't we have a wonderful last weekend?" Thank you, God, we did!

Through phone calls, it was decided that we would pick up their dog, Tuffy, and keep him until they were able to come home. Their neighbor, Ilene, helped us get in. Going into their home was probably one of the hardest things I had to do. Inside, God met us and allowed us to do the chores we needed to do.

We attended the funeral, picked up Tuffy, and headed home. Then and there we decided we needed to get a will done, which we did. After Linda and Chad got home, we returned and brought Tuffy home. Chad was certainly glad to see him.

Linda has taught me a lot during this lifetime. She has taught me how to mourn for and with others. I have always admired the way she made new traditions for her "newly formed" family. Also, I admired her continuing to travel and her involvement with MADD. God gave her the strength to do what I felt was impossible.

I know her story is true, as I have traveled some of the journey with and alongside her. As you read her book, I hope you get the message: God is faithful. He will go with us through the valley of death and beyond! I, too, look forward to the great reunion in heaven.

Brenda Kephart

Preface

∽

A friend stated that I needed to write a book. I just laughed inside, thinking: *Which episode of my life I would write about as my life has been one huge calamity?* I told her that maybe someday I would write about my experiences that have transpired over the years for my family. This would be included in the family history. Then, a couple of months after my friend's suggestion, my Sunday School teacher conveyed to the class that we should leave our story about what God has done in our lives to the next generation.

Reflecting over everything that has taken place in my adulthood, I need to let others beside just my family know how merciful God is even when life is in constant turmoil. I need to relate what God has done in my life of chaos, but I feel very deeply that I should continue to make known how driving under the influence of intoxicants will not only destroy but change a life forever. The scars from what a drunk driver did in my life are with me daily. Putting the details behind each scar all together in words is overwhelming, but, with God's help, I have followed my conscience after being nudged earlier to share my journey. I hope you see how God's strength has intervened in each episode.

Revealing my inner wounds over the past years is extremely difficult. However, they are a vital part of my story of how God has intervened. My inner struggles are essential that they be communicated. Being a reserved, independent woman and finding myself incredibly weak over the years, I could only depend on His listening ear, words of wisdom, and strength, which have continued to give me the courage required to get through a day, an hour, sometimes a minute. There have been some days that I needed His strength just to get through a second to continue with this journey. I know He gives me this strength only because He loves me. It will be an exciting day to take pleasure in the eternal home He has prepared for me and to see His face as well as thank Him for loving and caring about me.

I have envisioned myself hanging from a rope with Jesus's scarred hands as my lifeline, knowing countless numbers of times during my weaknesses I just wanted to let go and be able to bury the pain. Inside myself, I needed to keep a strong hold to the hand anchoring me because, without His power, I would never make it through the journey I have been asked to take.

A song from childhood says it all:

> Jesus loves me! This I know,
> For the Bible tells me so;
> Little ones to Him belong,
> They are weak, but He is strong.

We each deal with curves in our journey of life. Aside from the normal bends that have entered my life, I have had several switchback curves that have been extremely hard and dark, around which I was slow to maneuver. There have been times I felt that I would slip off and tumble down the cliff instead of completely making it around the curve in one piece. It has only been with Jesus hanging onto me that I have been able to manage each hairpin curve without plunging off the cliff. In the following pages, I will be sharing some of the tragedies that have invaded my adult life, which, with God's help, I have learned to live with. The memories of each one will never leave my mind.

I can visualize being on a winding road in the mountains and looking at the edge of each sharp curve with the river flowing below. Each tight curve represents a dark time in my life that was extremely hard to operate around in order to advance to the straight portion of the road again. There were several times that the straight section of the road was so short before entering into another hairpin curve. I am not sure what the next curve will be in my journey, but I continue to grasp onto Jesus's hand to guide me around it and help me to avoid tumbling over the cliff into the river below and drowning. He will help me through any new surprise that may assault my life. When I enter into these unknown curves where I could slip and fall, I will continually recall that Jesus held onto me tightly in the past, and He will not let me fall in the future either.

> "I will strengthen you, I will help you, I will uphold you with my victorious right hand." Isaiah 41:10b

PART ONE

"A happy family
is but an earlier heaven."

—George Bernard Shaw

Chapter 1

∽

I had purchased my first car, a 1966 baby blue Mustang, in July of 1967, and had stopped to show it to my dear friends, Brenda and Dan. Upon entering their house, I saw an unfamiliar young gentleman standing in the living room, who happened to be a coworker of Dan's. This stranger, Gary, had just arrived in Nampa, Idaho, from North Dakota earlier that month to attend Northwest Nazarene College (now University), which I was also attending. Following this unexpected meeting, Gary and I had our first date the following Saturday. We went to the car races in Meridian, and the love between the two of us began to blossom throughout the following months. On June 7, 1968, Gary Sundve and I, Linda Real, were united as one in the Fairview Nazarene Church in Nampa.

Joining the Sundve family was not only a pleasure but an honor, even though I did not meet Gary's parents face-to-face until two days before the wedding. From the telephone calls I had had with them previously, I was very anxious to meet them. In the previous months, Gary had related so many wonderful stories of his family that I could feel in numerous ways how close and fun the family was. Once I met them, I understood that closeness and how full of unselfish love they really were.

One of the attributes that drew me to Gary was his sense of humor and keenness of sharing stories that kept everyone laughing. The abundance of laughter from all the stories when the family was together was amazing. My ribs hurt from laughing. What a delight it was becoming a member of this marvelous, fun Christian family!

An extraordinary delight for me now was having someone to call "Dad." My father passed away when I was five from a heart attack at the young age of forty-seven in Wyoming, where I was born and lived for seven years. Having Gary's dad in my life helped fill several of the empty spaces that I had experienced growing up without a father in my young life. When visiting in their home, it was so enjoyable sitting at the dining room table for family devotions and having Dad open the Bible and read.

Gary and I stayed in Nampa until August 1970. Gary was a mechanic for the local school bus firm, and I was the billing clerk at the city sanitation company. In the early part of the summer that year, Gary received a call from the owner of the school bus company in Forest Grove, Oregon, offering him a position. We made a quick trip to Oregon on a weekend in July to see the facilities and the area, and to assess the offer, and then decided this would be an excellent advancement in Gary's employment.

Moving away from my mother for the first time was hard that late August day. However, Gary and I fell in love with an impressive western Oregon with its beautiful green fields, evergreen trees, the wonders of the Oregon coast and beaches, and the beauty of the snow-covered peaks of the Cascade Mountains.

That winter we were very fortunate to purchase an acre of land on a hillside with a marvelous view of the valley outside of Banks, where we built our first house the following year. The spectacular view of Mount Hood from the front window added to the beauty of the area, especially in the winter when the deep reddish colors of the sun were rising behind the mountain. This scene made an extraordinary framed picture in our window.

When Mother decided to move to Oregon from Idaho after her retirement in the summer of 1974, it was an added delight. She not only wanted to be near us, she was especially looking forward to being with another grandbaby when it was born since I was expecting our first child. She loved her grandbabies. When Chad joined the family on April 8, 1975, his birth was electrifying for everyone because from prior medical test the chances of children were very unlikely for Gary and me. Chad's birth was not only a great celebration but a special blessing from God and an answer to our prayer. Then we were blessed with our second son, Kirk, seventeen months later on September 29, 1976.

With all the events that had taken place since Gary and I had met nine years earlier in Nampa, we were now considered an "all-American family."

We were incredibly delighted with all that had transpired: We had children, a dachshund (Tuffy), a house of our own, each other, and 1966 baby blue Mustang.

Family Photo October 1977
Linda, Gary, Kirk, and Chad

PART TWO

"A box of new crayons! Now they're all pointy, lined up in order, bright and perfect. Soon they'll be a bunch of ground down, rounded, indistinguishable stumps, missing their wrappers and smudged with other colors. Sometimes life seems unbearably tragic."

—Bill Watterson

Chapter 2

᪥

The summer in 1977 had been very long for Gary. He was now a foreman for a large farm and produce corporation in the area, and it was nothing for him to work eighteen hours a day during the summer months. Gary took pleasure in his new job since he was raised on a farm in North Dakota and was now able to move back to his farming roots. After several years as a mechanic on school buses, both in Idaho and Oregon, he was excited to be offered the foreman position on the farm, but it was very hard for him to leave another job he also enjoyed. We were in prayer asking which path Gary should take. The doors opened, and Gary smoothly shifted to the foreman position on the farm and at the processing plant. After the filberts and walnuts were harvested in October of that year, there was a vast need for Gary to have a few days off to get rejuvenated from the long hours that he had endured over the past several months.

On a beautiful, sunny, autumn Saturday afternoon, November 19, 1977, we had a wonderful fried chicken dinner at my mother's (who made the best). It was near Thanksgiving, and we were heading east to Minnesota. Gary, Chad (who was now two), and Kirk (who was thirteen months), and I boarded a plane at Portland International Airport for a week's visit with Gary's family, who had moved from North Dakota to Minnesota in 1968.

Chad's excitement about flying on a "big" plane and seeing Grandma and Grandpa became very staggering for a two-year-old. With a change of planes in Spokane, Washington, we finally arrived at Minneapolis-St.

Paul International Airport around 9:30 that evening. Getting off the plane was so pleasant after keeping the boys entertained for three hours in the cramped space of the plane and walking down the ramp to the friendly faces of Gary's parents, Louis and Doris, and his brother Paul. Their welcoming voices and warm hugs were there to greet us at the arrival gate.

After retrieving the luggage from the carousel in the baggage claims area of the airport and loading it into the trunk of the gold 1973 Chevrolet Impala, we entered the car. The three men were secured in the front seat of the car: Paul in the driver's seat, Dad in the center, and Gary in the passenger seat. Everyone else entered into the back seat: Mom took the seat behind Gary with Chad on her lap, and I climbed into the car behind Paul with Kirk. We started the journey to their home in Dassel, which is about sixty miles west of Minneapolis on Highway 12.

There was the general catch-up conversation taking place in the car as we were traveling, including sharing the news that, in the previous week in North Dakota, Gary's cousin and her husband had been killed in a car accident, leaving behind five children. About halfway to Dassel, Chad was starting to get fussy after his long day, so it was necessary that Mom and I exchange boys. Immediately after the exchange, I looked up and saw two lights. No one in the car had time to say "watch out," "oh, no," or anything that you might say when an accident is about to happen. A split-second after seeing the lights at around 11:00 p.m. in Independence, Minnesota, my life had completely changed, and I have not been the same person since.

I was unconscious until I felt someone trying to move me. At that moment, I barely came to. In a state of bewilderment, I did not realize what was transpiring around me. The door was jammed on my side of the automobile, making it necessary to use the door on the opposite side to remove me, which meant going across Mom. Oh, to this day, I can feel the stillness of her body, yet at that instant, when I was being lifted out of wreckage, I was unaware of what that motionless body meant.

Once they were able to remove me from the car and put me on a gurney, I was lifted into the ambulance quickly, where I could hear Chad crying intensely. At that instant, all the pain in my body meant nothing. All I wanted to do at that moment was to embrace and comfort my hurting two-year-old who was crying so powerfully. But my body was incapable of letting me do so. In all my anguish, the only thing I could do for my son was to try to utter a few comforting words to let him know I was there. Chad was on a shelf area of the ambulance, but with all the commotion, sirens, and confusion that were encircling us, I doubt that he even heard the few words of reassurance I was trying to impart to him.

Within seconds, a policeman came to the ambulance asking me how many people were in our car. When I tried to count, I was unable to because I was confused. I gave a number that I thought was correct, but days later at the hospital I realized it had been incorrect. To know my body and mind had been in such a state of trauma that it was even impossible to count really bothered me. With the brain trauma, it took three months before I realized that the exchange of the boys had taken place just seconds before our car was hit. I thought that I was holding Kirk at the time of the accident, but all the reports stated differently.

Dad was also lifted on a gurney into the ambulance with Chad and me. He was placed next to me, and his intense groans pierced my ears. I heard the paramedics say that his legs were severed. This was inconceivable to my ears! Chad's cries, Dad's groans, and the paramedics' words in the ambulance were branded into my mind that night, and I have never been able to wipe them away.

Quickly the doors of the ambulance slammed shut, and we started racing down the highway for the hospital in Minneapolis with sirens blaring. The paramedics were busy cutting my clothes off to get to my injuries. While I lay there helpless hearing more sirens in the area, the last thought before going unconscious was that the others were not injured quite as badly and that we needed to get to the hospital first.

After going unconscious in the ambulance, I was unaware of anything around me as we arrived at the hospital. I was taken to the Intensive Care Unit (ICU). Later, while being wheeled down the hall to surgery, in my dazed state of mind and not knowing what was taking place, the hospital chaplain halted the bed and conveyed horrendous words to me: Gary, Kirk, Paul, Mom, and Dad were dead. Dad had passed away in the ambulance en route to the hospital. Despite the state of my body and mind, the words were horrifying (I cannot even write about that moment). Even though I was in shock, once I heard those profound words—that five people I loved were dead and two of those people were my husband and son—they became so real to my boggled mind. No words can even describe what I just heard; it was a miracle that I was sedated for surgery when I heard them.

At about the same time that I was being taken to surgery and was told about the deaths, my sister-in-law Mary, Paul's wife, was awakened with a knock at their door in Dassel. The police were there to break the horrible news to her. Mary, who was pregnant with their third child, had stayed behind at Mom and Dad's house with their two young sons: Brent, who would turn three in a few days on Thanksgiving, and Bryce, who was one. In addition, so that both Mom and Dad could go to the airport, Mary was also caring for Dad and Mom's daughter, Linda, a special needs girl, and Mom's sister, Martha, with Parkinson's. I must incorporate here that Linda was mentally unable to understand what was taking place: One day Mom and Dad were there, and the next day she never saw them again.

Mary had so many unpleasant items that hit her plate at that moment. Not only did she just find out about the loss of her husband and the other family members, she had to start making those ugly telephone calls to inform others of this horrible wreck and deaths that occurred, including my mother back in Oregon.

Once my mother received Mary's call, she informed the pastor of our church in Hillsboro of the collision. He broke the news to the congregation that Sunday morning; I was informed later by friends that the service was very somber. Gary and I were active in the church; Gary was on the church board, and I was treasurer, plus the majority of our friends attended the church. The congregation started praying for Chad's and my healing, and in particular, that both of us would survive for each other.

Another person that Mother contacted that morning was Gary's boss, Dwayne, who had become very close to Gary not only as a boss but as a friend. Dwayne took charge of making the arrangements for Mother to fly to Minnesota and took her to the airport later that day in Portland. My sister, Peggy, flew from Boise, Idaho, and they arrived at the hospital late Sunday night. In the early days after the wreck, Gary's boss was the key person who stepped in and took charge of all the needed paperwork for Social Security survivor benefits, arrangements for the cemetery plots, a lawyer for the estate, and so many other necessary tasks in Oregon that needed to be addressed that I was unable to perform.

I had been admitted to North Memorial Hospital with the following injuries: multiple soft tissue contusions; nasal fracture; mandible fracture; T-type supracondylar fracture of the left femur, extending into the knee joint (; misalignment of the left leg; and a mild cerebral concussion. The first few days were very fuzzy in ICU, where they kept me because of the "stormy course"(from the medical report my body was having difficulty due to the blunt chest trauma, which can affect any one of chest wall and thoracic cavity causing death).

The first surgery performed on me was the installation of a skeletal traction into the upper part of the tibia to assist in pulling the alignment of the leg to the proper position before the fractures of the femur and knee could be addressed. It was not until the following day that they discovered the broken jaw. I can remember an ICU nurse asking me if my jaw always hung sideways. Once they discovered that it was broken, they took me back into surgery for installation of arch bars on my teeth in order to hold my jaw in place for healing.

I was released from ICU on Tuesday, three days after the collision, and placed in a standard hospital room, where I was now bedridden, having to lay flat on my back because of the rod through my tibia that was attached in the air to the traction equipment. The doctors stated that this could take six to eight weeks to correct the alignment. With my teeth wired shut, I could only drink soft, watery food through a straw and mumble my words when I spoke. I had to rely on the nursing staff and others to take care of all my daily needs. But with all the physical pain and daily requirements that I now faced, they all became insignificant and minor compared to the emotional journey that I was now entering into from the loss of my family.

Chad had been somewhat responsive at the scene with his crying, but, shortly after arrival at the hospital, he was unresponsive with his pupils widely dilated and eye movement in opposite directions from each other. In addition, he was becoming markedly less mobile. The doctor's report stated, "I found him to be basically flaccid (lifeless) except for the eye movement. His respiratory efforts were very poor, and his color was not good and blood pressure was seemingly falling. It was my feeling that he probably was in some form of status epilepiticus (a life-threatening condition in which the brain is in a state of persistent seizure lasting longer than thirty minutes) . . ." Further reports stated that "all this was adding to his neurologic deterioration. An emergency intubation was carried out and an intravenous medication was used to bring control of his seizure. With this regime, his seizuring stopped, and he began to show withdrawal type movements of his limbs." He had a computerized axial tomography (CAT) scan that showed no intracranial hemorrhage. Because of his head injury, his balance was not stable. He was kept immobile for a few days with a net over his crib, where he remained hospitalized until the day after Thanksgiving, the twenty-fifth of November.

I cannot imagine what the first twenty-four hours at the hospital must have been like for Chad with the strange faces and the poking and prodding of the nurses and doctors. The hospital surroundings were such an unfamiliar environment for a two-year-old to be alone without his mom or dad at his side to hold and comfort him through his pain. His cries for a little blue bear and blanket were met when they were found in the wrecked car by a dear friend of the family, Cliff. Yes, the stuff blue bear and the soft blanket were the security that helped this boy through a day of mystery until his grandma arrived. Peggy and Mother both related later that when he saw Grandma, he cried "Grandma, Grandma" and held out his arms. What a scene that had to be!

A memorial service for the family was being planned in Dassel, where Dad, Mom, and Paul were all employed in different positions by the school district. The whole family was well-known in this small community and finding a location that would be able to handle the expected crowd was vital. The decision was made for the service to be held in the school gymnasium in Dassel, the best facility for the family's final service together. The memorial service took place on the afternoon of November 23, the day before Thanksgiving, with the gymnasium crowded. Among those in attendance were my mother and sister, as well as Gary's boss and his wife who had flown in from Oregon.

Being alone in the hospital during the memorial service, trying to visualize what the service was like, was not an easy undertaking. It is not a common occurrence in your life for a memorial service to occur for five people you love dearly and be denied the opportunity to hear the last words spoken about each one and have comforting words ministered to you. Even though I could not be there in person, I was at peace knowing each one loved the Lord and were now celebrating in heaven together. Just to know that Kirk was laid to rest in his father's arms helped, as he was buried with Gary. That picture in my thoughts was extremely important and comforting for me while lying there in my agonized state of mind—alone.

The Sundve Family's Memorial Service,
November 23, 1977, Dassel, Minnesota

I had Gary and Kirk flown back to Oregon, where a service for both was held for our friends at the Hillsboro Nazarene Church on Tuesday, November 29. Since being part of the planning was impossible for me, I needed to depend on others to make the arrangements for this service. Even though I could not be there in person, the people back home in Oregon were exceptional for asking for my input. My pastor's wife, Carroll Miller, called me at the hospital to get suggestions of songs I would like included. My mind was empty or may have been too full of grief to even think of one song. I was so glad to be able to depend on the wisdom of others during this time and thankful that God used so many people to have the correct songs chosen, including the song Gary sung as a solo the last Sunday he attended church before the accident at the twenty-fifth anniversary of the church, "How Firm A Foundation." The words recited by Reverend Wally Miller, our pastor, were so truthful and meaningful; I am thankful people in the church took the time to make sure the service was taped for me and Chad to listen to later.

The fourth verse from "How Firm a Foundation," written by John Rippon in 1787, was always a comfort to me later:

> When through the deep waters I call thee to go,
> The rivers of woe shall not thee overflow;
> For I will be with thee, thy troubles to bless,
> And sanctify to thee thy deepest distress.

The hurt of not being able to say my final good-byes to Gary and Kirk in either service still stings. I read later that it is part of the grieving process to say those final good-byes. That was stolen from me. I have always felt so cheated.

Newspaper article written by Jim Adams, *Death in a family color Dassel Thanksgiving*, Minneapolis Star November 23, 1977 pages 1A and 12A.

Chapter 3

❧

The days in the hospital were very long even though there were scores of events occurring each day. While lying there, I was trying to comprehend what had taken place that night of the accident. When I was in ICU, I had been told that a drunk driver crashed into our car head-on. It was when the insurance adjustor visited me and revealed further details of the accident that the reality of what occurred that night pierced me and crushed me deeply. A twenty-six-year-old single man had been celebrating at a birthday party. He had stopped at a local bar before heading home alone in his intoxicated state. He came around the curve in his 1972 dark green Oldsmobile on the wrong side of the highway at a high rate of speed, striking our car.

When this information was revealed, this became a wreck to me and not an accident because it could have been prevented. There is a difference! The twenty-six-year-old also was killed instantly. Consequently, six people lost their lives that night because someone thought they could drive after drinking. Upon realizing that this could have been prevented, and that my family members' deaths and Chad's and my suffering were all in vain, the anger started to swell up inside me.

Two policemen who were at the scene of the wreck also came to visit and confirmed that the two cars were just four inches from being directly head-on at the time of impact. The twenty-six-year-old had driven his car completely on the wrong side of the road. Since none of us had seat belts on, which was not required in 1977, it was also a big concern to me, and

I needed to know if they might have saved lives. The policemen assured me that if the lap seat belts or if child car seats (they were not the safest back in 1977 nor were they required) were used, it would not have made any difference in this wreck. The intensity of the collision had forced the engine of our car into the front seat and the luggage in the trunk was crushed.

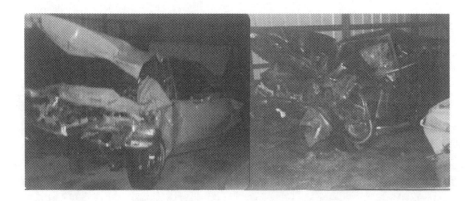

1973 Chevrolet 1972 Oldsmobile
The two cars involved in the wreck on November 19, 1977

Being associated with an International Denominational church is wonderful. I was eighteen hundred miles away from my local church, pastor, and friends, but there were pastors, local church people, and people in the community who were so wonderful to visit a suffering stranger. A special person was Norman Bloom, the Nazarene Minnesota District Superintendent at that time. His regular visits, words, and prayers became tremendously crucial to me in my anguish. Norman has continued to minister to me over the years with his wonderful Christmas letters, which are a special blessing along with knowing that he still cares after all these years.

The hospital chaplain visited me at the end of every day. I have to truly say those where very difficult times for me. I appreciated his concern, words, and prayers, but every time I was in his presence, it reminded me of the night he had given me the horrible news about my family. Even though I was heavily sedated that night, I still remember his presence and words. I am ashamed that I could not get beyond that point throughout his visits.

Nights were very lonely as I lay in bed after everyone had gone for the day, hearing only the ordinary bells and the nurses' voices coming from the hospital hall. I would look at the door, yearning and hoping that Gary would enter to visit me. There were times when I would look at the empty bed in the room and desire that he could be there healing too with me.

During those vacant nights, I picked up the Bible that was in the drawer next to the bed. I turned to the Psalms since I knew that Gary was reading the Psalms in his daily devotions at the time of his death. I not only needed the Psalmist's assurance; reading those words helped me feel closer to Gary knowing that I was reading the same words that he had read in the weeks before. Also, one of Gary's favorite chapters in the Bible was Psalms 1.

Even though there were several local people in the community visiting me, it was so good when the cards and especially the telephone calls started coming from my friends back home in Oregon. I still cannot imagine how hard it must have been for them to make those calls, but to hear a familiar voice and to know that people were praying meant so much. There were several people who related to me later that they were extremely scared to telephone because they did not know what to say. There are no magic words that can take the emotional pain away, even though that would have been nice. To know that I was loved and cared for alleviated some of the pain at the moment.

I cannot help but mention those liquid meals and especially the awful milkshake each day with a raw egg (yuck) that I needed for the extra protein. This became the common meal that I had to drink through the straw each day. As a side note, the hospital nutritionist and kitchen did try their best with the liquid diet. On Thanksgiving Day, they watered down the potatoes and gave me turkey gravy to drink so that I could have some sort of Thanksgiving dinner.

Chad could be released from the hospital since his balance was adequate. On Friday, November 25, he was discharged, and Mother and Peggy brought him directly upstairs to the seventh floor to room 704. I had not seen my precious son in six days, and the emotional and physical hurt that both of us had endured separately was inconceivable. I was looking forward to seeing his smiling face, hearing his voice, and being able to touch his warm body again. Most important was being able to observe with my own eyes that he was physically sound.

The mental picture of my two-year-old son standing at my hospital door in his yellow and orange sweatshirt and brown corduroy jeans, looking so pale and puzzled, is still wedged in my memory. He stood motionless in the doorway and stared, so overwhelmed at seeing his mother in those circumstances: The equipment holding her leg in the air, her bruises, and the wires on her teeth. The imagine Chad was seeing at that moment must had been hard and frightening. I assured him in my mumbled voice that it was okay and held out my arms. Finally, I was able to touch and feel his little arms around me. Oh, what a reunion in that room that afternoon! Most of all, having him close to me again and seeing that he was thriving was beyond words. Then the awful question came, "Where is Daddy?" I remembered looking out the window at a pond with several kids playing ice hockey and telling him that Daddy and Kirk were now in heaven with Jesus.

Peggy and Mother rented a small boarding room that was close to the hospital and traveled back and forth by taxi each day. The days in Minnesota were unusually cold during this time. The temperature was in the minuses, and the wind chill made the temperatures even colder. They said going from the taxi into the hospital entrance caught their breath every morning.

Into the third week of my recovery, my sister needed to return to her job in Idaho, and the decision had to be made about Chad and Mother. Peggy, Mother, and other family members were discussing that Chad would go home with Peggy, and Mother would stay with me until I could be released. In my thoughts, I did not want Chad to take part in another unknown circumstance in his life without me. I knew that this is what should happen since Mother could not manage both of us in Minneapolis by herself. We discussed the situation with the doctor, wanting to find out the status of my progress and if there was any possibility of transferring me to a hospital in Oregon.

Every few days, the hospital radiation staff transported the mobile X-ray machine into my room for new pictures of my leg and knee to determine my current progress. The latest X-rays revealed widening of the condylar fragments in the femur, which meant that the femur bone was broken in several parallel places and were widening. As a result, I entered surgery again at the start of my fourth week. At this point, I had a threaded 1/7-inch K Hagey pin with nuts and washers applied to maintain the positioning of the widened intercondylar fragments. Even though the alignment was not correct as yet, the widening of the fragments into the femur took priority. The doctor determined that the alignment would be adequate and removed the rod in the tibia bone that was connected to the skeletal traction. This enabled a full-leg cast, hip to toes, to be applied. The doctors also determined that this would be an ideal time to remove the arch braces from my teeth while I was still sedated.

Even with the dreadful news of the widening of the fragments in the femur and not having the alignment complete, the surgery that took place that morning now allowed me to go home with Chad and Mother, and Peggy could go to her job and family in Idaho. Again, God's miraculous hand was intervening in my body to prevent Chad from having to face another situation without me.

The next few days were filled with major changes and challenges in preparing for the trip back to Oregon. The first challenge was sitting up after lying flat for over three weeks. The wonder of being able to eat solid food again had sounded so good after having to drink my meals, but eating was extremely limited for several weeks after the braces were removed. Those favorite foods I was craving would have to continue to wait.

I attended a quick, one-time physical therapy session to learn how to use crutches with the heavy, full-leg cast. I remember the therapist telling me that the bad leg goes down like the "baddies," and the good leg goes up the steps like the "goodies." Those words always came to me when I started going up and down the stairs later with the crutches. But at this time, I needed to use the wheelchair to keep my leg elevated and only used the crutches where the wheelchair could not go.

Chapter 4

&

The arrangements for flying home were completed, including the van that Cliff, a close friend of the family, had obtained to take Mother, Peggy, Chad, and me to the airport. On Saturday, December 17, four weeks to the day since the wreck, I left North Memorial Hospital for Minneapolis-St. Paul International airport. Even with the excitement of returning home after being hospitalized for four weeks, I had mixed feelings. The greatest fear was that my frail, weak body would not make the long journey to the airport, onto the plane, and home to Oregon. At the hospital it was a challenge getting me into the van with the heavy cast, and the thought of doing this over again onto the planes was overwhelming.

As we left the hospital in the van, on the roadway a second fear embraced me. I had not even thought about the fear of riding in another vehicle. With the weakness of my body and this fear within me, pulling away from the secure hospital boundaries that Saturday morning into another unknown was terrifying.

Cliff, Mother, Peggy, Chad, and I arrived at the Minneapolis-St Paul International Airport. There were no wheelchairs in the airport with a leg extension so that my leg could be elevated. This was a must since there was no bend at the knee with the full cast and bolt. So, with the creative minds around, Peggy and Cliff created a makeshift extension using a crutch so that I could use the wheelchair and keep my leg elevated. My body was too weak to attempt walking on the crutches for the first time in the long corridors of the terminal.

Cliff and his family had done so much for my family and me during my hospital stay. Most of all, he was very close to the Sundve family after having lived with Mom and Dad for a period of time. Gary stated many times that he had considered Cliff as his other brother. With many hugs and tears flowing, saying good-bye to this special family member was extremely difficult at the boarding gate. Once the final good-byes were uttered, I was transferred onto a special narrow board seat and wheeled into the aircraft for the first part of my journey back home to Oregon.

The flight attendants were so compassionate when they saw me coming into the airplane on this special board with my sister holding my leg. They had unoccupied seats in first class in the first row and made sure I sat in one instead of trying to get me back into the coach area. They propped my cast leg on pillows and were able to locate seats around me for Chad, Mother, and Peggy so that we could be together on the first part of our flight to Spokane.

Spokane International Airport brought back memories of when Gary, the boys, and I had landed there one month earlier. It might seem strange to most, but the scene that stood out so strongly in my mind while I sat and waited for the next plane to Portland was when I used the restroom to change Kirk's diaper for the last time.

Gary's boss, Dwayne, met us at Portland International Airport that evening for the journey to our home in Banks. There, Peggy's husband, Roger, and children, Barbara and Bruce, plus my neighbor and dear friend, Ilene Sheeley, were waiting.

The trip back home that day had been very long and exhausting. Once I was carried into the house and placed into the wheelchair, the welcoming sight of family members and my dear friend along with their hugs and cheerful voices invigorated me. The house looked wonderful. A decorated Christmas tree sat in the corner of the living room with gifts underneath, and numerous Christmas goodies on the table that dear friends and neighbors had provided. Knowing that we were loved, the long day ended with meaning. Being home finally was so good.

But later that evening, when I wheeled myself down the hall to Kirk's bedroom, oh, how the emptiness for my missing baby invaded me. There was his crib, stuffed toys, and little clothes hanging in the closet, but no baby. Kirk had occupied that room for thirteen short months, but yet there were so many memories contained within those four walls.

After the extremely long day of traveling, I was not only fatigued, but my body was experiencing tremendous weakness from the first day out of the hospital in four weeks. I had to try to get some rest and went to bed with assistance.

Here I was, lying alone on my sheepskin with my leg elevated on a stack of pillows, in the bed that I had shared with Gary for nine-and-a-half years. The emptiness that I felt from not being able to snuggle up to his warm body again was dreadful and created an exceedingly long, restless night. In 1968, we had become one; now, one of us was not there anymore. The loss of that oneness left a huge hole within me. Gary had been the "sunshine in my life." Now the sunshine was gone, and the darkness was entering me.

Chapter 5

❧

Being home again was tremendous, even though it meant the beginning of a strange journey within familiar surroundings. It was a trip that I did not want to enter or even acknowledge. Since I still needed assistance with my physical needs and with taking care of Chad, Mother temporarily moved in with us for the next four months.

It was now the week before Christmas. Friends had provided magnificent gifts under the tree, including items that Chad had on his wish list. Also, one evening during that week, a group of friends from church surprised me with their presence and sang carols of Jesus's birth. Just seeing their wonderful, familiar faces again and hearing the amazing Christmas songs really touched my heart. Even with all the love that had been shown by friends, Christmas celebrations were empty without having my entire family present. Christmas celebration was not the same, and never has been.

This was going to be Gary's, the boys', and my first Christmas at home with just the four of us, as we had always gone away for Christmas. But now we wanted to start developing our own Christmas traditions as a family in our home. I had prepared several Christmas items before we left on our trip to Minnesota, including painting wooden Christmas decorations of Disney characters that I knew the boys would enjoy seeing on the tree.

In addition, I had Chad and Kirk's picture taken for our Christmas card. The cards were not finished when we left on our trip. I did not see them until I got home, and, sadly, Gary never saw them. Mailing those cards to family and friends with the boys' happy smiles for everyone to enjoy was going to be a delight. But now there was no way I could mail them with one of the boys now deceased. I was very proud of my boys and wanted to share them with others, but instead of bringing joy, these cards brought great sorrow. The Christmas dreams I had a few weeks before had been shattered to pieces in a split-second by a drunk driver.

Kirk and Chad's Christmas card 1977

Those early months at home were extremely difficult. Just getting up every morning was an emotional journey for me. There were so many times I wanted—and maybe I did—to pull the covers over my head and forget that another day was beginning. I also had wonderful dreams of Gary and wanted to stay within the dream world instead of waking up to real life.

Before the wreck, mornings were a special time for Gary and me, which probably had a great influence on why I did not want to tackle another day now. I always enjoyed fixing Gary's breakfast and packing his lunch. Most enjoyable was when we took our second cup of coffee to the living room to have a quiet time together without the boys interrupting our conversation. There was such deep desire within me to be able to have those quiet times back each morning with the man I loved, but now I was forced into starting the day without him.

A few days after Christmas, I began physical therapy to regain the strength in my leg. Since it was still difficult for me to move outside the house, home therapy sessions were scheduled. The morning before leaving the hospital in Minnesota, I felt a sore developing on the back side of my upper thigh from the cast even though it had been on only a few days. So the nurse attached a piece of soft wool material to the cast in hopes that it would help. But once home, the pain from the sore increased, and since it was on the back side of my thigh, I was unable to examine it. In one of my home therapy sessions in late December, I asked the therapist to look at it. She discovered an open sore that looked poorly and called the doctor immediately. She was so considerate and drove me the twenty miles to the doctor, who removed the plaster cast and fitted me with an upper thigh fiberglass brace that hinged to the plaster cast on the tibia. The physician told me that if the sore had gone another day or two without attention, I would have ended up back in the hospital.

February 14, Valentine's Day, was a very lonely day. Every year, Gary gave me an amazing card with a handwritten note of appreciation and love. Now this day was lacking that special card. To add to the loneliness, Mother and I had taken Chad to the barber shop for his hair cut. While I waited in the car until they were finished, the company pickup that Gary drove to work pulled into the parking lot. Seeing the vehicle for the first time after Gary's death with someone else behind the wheel cut into my heart, and the tears flowed.

Also in February, the telephone call came from my sister-in-law Mary in Minnesota, saying that she had given birth to a baby girl. The picture of not having Paul at her side was disturbing because Paul really wanted to have a daughter. Now she was born, but Paul was not there to hold this precious little girl. The one thing that Mary could give their daughter was the name Paula, in memory of her father.

On February 24, the leg cast was removed, and on March 9, I was again admitted to the hospital for surgery to remove the bolt in my lower femur, which was visible through the skin. I continued with physical therapy sessions the next two months to gain additional motion in my knee after the pin and cast were removed. To increase the strength in the leg that had atrophied. To learn how to walk again (this was really a challenge, but a wonderful challenge). Even after the therapy session discontinued, I had to continue to use a cane to assist in my balance and help when the knee would slip. Regaining my physical strength and learning to walk on my own after the wreck took eight long months. This long journey consisted of being bedridden to a wheelchair and then to crutches, and, finally, a cane.

Since I had not yet had my broken nose addressed and was having difficulty breathing and could only open my mouth partially from the broken jaw, I saw an ear, nose, and throat specialist, who recommended that I undergo an intranasal reconstruction after my leg was stable. This procedure would relieve the nasal obstruction from the septal bucking from the nasal fracture. At this time, I had fifty percent of my full excursion in opening my mouth, which he felt would improve with time. On May 10, I was admitted again to the hospital for the nasal septal reconstruction surgery.

The days seemed very long, especially with not being able to physically do the things that I wanted to do outside of my home and having to do so many things that I did not want to do. I did resume my treasurer's duties for the church again in January, which was something I could do from my wheelchair at home and enabled me to direct my mind on other things a few hours each week. Being housebound did not give me any relief from the grief that was in my walls at home. Mother and my friend tried to teach me different handiwork to take my mind off things. Some days this worked; other days, it was hard to focus on it.

In the summer of 1978, the settlement of Dad and Mom's estate needed to be attended to and closed on. It was a strange that their daughters-in-law had to take charge of this task. With the death of their two sons, Gary and Paul, and their only daughter with special needs, Mary and I were next in line to perform this assignment. Knowing this should not be solely Mary's responsibility to tackle this enormous chore, I was thankful that my leg allowed me to fly with Chad to Minnesota late in July to assist with the preparation for the estate sale in August.

This chore was not simple. We had to go through Mom and Dad's belongings and determine what was saleable, what should be kept in the family, and what needed to be thrown out. While touching their possessions, our memories flowed back to the days we had spent together in their home as a family and all the laughter we shared. During this time, the reality of the loss of my other family members, Mom, Dad, and Paul became so strong, and the grieving for them began.

The wonderful people in the community, who assisted us before as well as on the day of the sale, relieved some of the stress from Mary and me and were vital in making the sale a success. However, the day of the sale brought troublesome feelings for me, as it was difficult seeing their possessions now being owned by someone else. With the sale of their belongings, my in-laws, who I loved and had so much fun with, were now drawing further away from me. It seemed like only yesterday when I had married into this family, and now this family was starting to disappear.

The days had been long, demanding, and emotionally draining. Preparing for the sale and the sale itself made it essential for both Mary and me to have a change of surroundings. Mary wanted to drive Chad and me back to Oregon. How I was looking forward to spending this time with her and the children and being in another setting. There were several who thought we were silly to undertake such a trip, and maybe we were. But this silliness was the therapy and the needed change both of us needed after all that we had endured the last few months.

The venture included a tent trailer, four children, ages three and under (Mary's three children—Brent, Bryce, and Paula—and Chad), plus a teenage girl who would assist with the children when Mary returned to Minnesota from Oregon. To help visualize what we looked like, we had a Jeep Cherokee with seven people inside; boxes of mementos that I was taking home from Mom and Dad's tied on top; and the luggage, food, and other essentials in the tent trailer that were being towed. We headed down the highway to Oregon via Nebraska, Wyoming, Utah, and Idaho, stopping at a campground each night and rolling up the tent on the trailer. This venture was a trip that Mary and I still talk and laugh about; it was the therapy that we both needed.

Chapter 6

⤚

To add to the complexities of everything that was happening, I had to enter the legal system, which was all new and strange to me. I did not expect the process to be as complicated and time consuming as it was. The three-inch file that contains all the paperwork relating to the wreck, including the lawyer's papers, the hospital bills, and the doctor and police reports are still in my files. Since the twenty-six-year-old driver who had crashed into Dad and Mom's car was uninsured, Mom and Dad's car insurance took effect, paying the medical, funeral, and other settlement expenses.

Being an Oregon resident involved in a wreck in Minnesota created additional insurance and legal problems: The law in Minnesota was different from Oregon's law for collecting the uninsured portion of motor insurance. In Minnesota, all insurances policies of the parties involved are allowed to be stacked, and in Oregon, only the main insurance policy of the car involved is valid. With the different state laws, the courts had to determine which state law would preside. The courts final decision was that Minnesota law would prevail since the wreck took place in Minnesota. As a result, the Oregon insurance policies would be stacked with the other party's insurance policies, according to the Minnesota law.

I had to hire three lawyers, one in Minnesota, two in Oregon (one for the estate, which went very smoothly, and another to handle the legalities of the Oregon insurance and to intercede between me and my lawyer in Minnesota). The legal settlement continued for three years with an arbitration hearing held in Minnesota toward the end that included all parties. When the day arrived in December 1980 for the signing of the last legal paper, it was not only a day of relief, but a day of celebration. This chapter could be put to rest.

The day of the arbitration hearing regarding how the insurance dollars should be divided based on each loss was very difficult for me. I do not like this type of circumstance, especially with ones I love. As part of the pre-arbitration, Chad and I had to go back to Minnesota in November 1979 to be examined by doctors that the insurance company had chosen.

After my orthopedic examination in Minnesota, the doctor stated in his report to the lawyers: "The patient has an obvious permanent medical impairment and loss of physical function to the left lower extremity as a whole. I think the patient runs a significant risk of persistent arthritic changes in the left knee with obvious evidence of patellofemoral arthritis present already. The need for further surgery in the future cannot be excluded . . . I feel the patient has a 30% permanent physical impairment and loss of physical function to the left lower extremity as a whole." The report also stated that my walk had an obvious limp due to the half-inch that was lost in my left leg from supracondylar fracture. Note: A supracondylar fracture is a very complex injury with numerous complications such as mal alignment, flexion contractures, stiffness, and limb length discrepancies. Since the femur is such a strong bone, it takes tremendous force to cause a femur fracture especially above the knee.

Chad's examination with the neurologist surgeon in Minneapolis was very positive—just what a parent wants to hear. The doctor felt from all the signs that Chad had made a complete recovery from his head injury and no other CAT or electroencephalogram (EEG) would be needed. This was good news since head injuries could cause medical problems later on, according to what I had heard and read. But even with the good news, probably due to my mother's instinct, I lived in fear over the years that something would develop.

Mary and I had ridden together from Dassel to the arbitration hearing that morning in Minneapolis. We had meetings with our respective lawyers, but it was so good when we came back together. We both felt peace and calmness from God, which enabled us to sit with the lawyers and the arbitration panel and listen to each case as it was presented.

PART THREE

"Every man has his secret sorrows which the world knows not; and often times we call a man cold when he is only sad."

—Henry Wadsworth Longfellow

Chapter 7

❧

Everyone encounters grief in numerous ways; none are identical or comparable. Also, the grieving timeline is never similar. I felt so weighted down with grief over the loss of five people; losing my other half and love and becoming a widow at thirty years old; being forced to become a single mom; becoming head of the household and making all the major decisions alone; losing a child; becoming a single person again; losing my in-laws, who I had a special love for; my physical injuries and dealing with the endless physical pain; and trying to tackle all the emotions from the trauma of a tragic wreck. Plus, I was angry that my family was killed in a wreck that could have been prevented.

For one individual to be handed a plate that is piled high to overflowing with countless major life-changing events at one time is extremely uncommon. Worse yet, without knowing how to even grasp, prioritize, and address even one of the events that occurred. I was overwhelmed with the plate that was handed to me on November 19, 1977, and was only able to take baby bites from the plate in order to even survive. There were days when I felt buried in the pile of unwanted, major events that I did not desire or choose but were forced upon me by a drunk driver. These were now the chief ingredients of my life. With so many key episodes entering my life at one time, my grieving process has taken much longer. Today the plate is still not empty.

I have felt so slow in trying to empty this plate. There have been days when I wonder why it is taking me so long. But after reading several articles, I found that the full plate of major changes and the effect it has on a person's life, plus my response in dealing with grief that included additional setbacks, is completely normal in the mourning process for *traumatic and sudden* deaths of family members along with dealing with a harrowing wreck. I realized that I was not dealing with the normal grief that everyone deals with at some point in life. I also realized that it was even hard for people to minister to me because of the complexities that traumatic and sudden deaths have on an individual, which is probably why I had to withdraw into myself.

A traumatic and sudden death influences the grieving person to be at a much greater risk for enduring subsequent complicated mourning. But to deal with several traumatic and sudden deaths at once made the mourning even worse, sometimes to being unbearable. One day I might mourn for one and the next day for another, but most days I mourned for five. I was buried in grief that only God was able to carry me though one day at a time. Under no circumstances could I manage the numerous traumatic deaths and events that encircled me from this tormenting wreck in my own power.

The emotional scars I acquired outweighed the physical scars I acquired from the wreck, and they were much harder to deal with. The emotional scars have taken many years to learn how to live with. Conversing about my physical condition to friends was much easier than about my emotional condition because dealing with the wreck and my losses were very difficult to share. Even to begin to try to understand myself was very hard, and I knew others would not understand the massive losses and how they affected my life. Time had passed, and people thought that time should have healed me and that everything should be fine by now. I was constantly being told how strong I was; I guess I did not want to disappoint people by letting them know I was falling apart inside because it would show my weaknesses. So I disguised myself behind a smiling mask.

I am so thankful that God has always been beside me. He does understand my weaknesses and has carried and is still carrying me through so many circumstances that otherwise I would never have been able to survive on my own. He is my anchor. Even after thirty-three years since the wreck, there is not a day that goes by that a physical or emotional scar does not creep in to remind me of that awful split-second in 1977. I wish this inner tormenting could be over and done with, but I am afraid that I am unable to wash away physical or emotional scars—they are permanent! You can try to hide them with make-up, but this is only temporary. Scars modify your life in countless ways, forcing you to learn to live with the changes. A person never completely gets over what caused the alterations. This is the scar.

Over the years, hearing sirens have given me flashbacks of that awful night of the wreck, forcing me to remember the cries of my two—year-old or the groans of my father-in-law or feeling the excruciating pain from my injuries. After several years of enduring these flashbacks, in an attempt to alleviate those revolting images and sounds from my mind, I pray for the individual who is in the ambulance that God would meet whatever needs they may have at that moment.

The two lights that I saw that horrible night of the wreck continues in my mind today and contribute to the incredible fear that challenges me in a car. Traveling on a two-lane highway can be very tough at times even today. If a car is coming toward the center line, my stomach leaps and the fear from wondering if they will stay on their side of the highway grips my whole body and mind. One night about two years after the wreck, I was coming home on a dark, rainy night. The headlights from every car I met felt like they were on my side of the road. I was so frightened that I pulled over onto the shoulder and prayed that I would make it home. My first instinct was to grab Chad, who was in the backseat, and walk home. But God guided the car home safely that night. The wreck also made me a very nervous passenger. I know what can take place in a split-second and do not want to ever experience it again or have anyone else experience such an awful disaster.

Those two lights also haunt me during my sleep. Not only having to go through this dreadful wreck and having all the memories that are associated with it, but my nights were filled with dreams of that event. I was living with this horrible occurrence day and night. I would wake up from those ghoulish nightmares, screaming and shaking, and walked the floor to calm my trembling body. The following morning after a dreadful nightmare, my voice would often be hoarse from screaming.

Those monster nightmares went on for five years after the wreck, leaving me exhausted after each one. I prayed over and over that God would release me from those ugly dreams. Finally, God intervened. After being awakened by yet another horrendous nightmare, I got up, went through my routine walk around the house, and returned to bed, sensing that it would be all right and falling back to sleep. Suddenly, I was awakened by another nightmare a few minutes later. Lying there in tears, I wondered how much longer I would have to endure these nightmares. Suddenly, I saw a bright light at the foot of my bed with Jesus standing with his arms open wide. He said, "Fear not, for I am with you. Be not dismayed, for I am your God. I will strengthen you. I will help you. I will uphold you . . ." And that was my last horrible nightmare of the car wreck! Praise to God for healing me and giving me His comforting words from Isaiah 41:10.

Five years passed before I could embrace a baby without that awful heavy emotional pain invading me—the pain of yearning to have my own baby to cuddle and laugh with. A friend of mine, Karan, was expecting triplets, and her husband, Jim, was diagnosed with cancer when the first baby was to come home from the hospital. I longed to assist with taking care of the babies, but I could not do it in my own power. I needed God's healing. Praise God, He gave me the strength to lend a helping hand to those three wonderful lives.

Barrenness invaded my body from Kirk's loss. Only a mother who has lost a child can understand. I had carried that little boy in my body for nine months until he could draw his first breath. I felt his movements within me, heard his first cry, heard his first word, and watched him take his first step. And now he had vanished. I have often wondered what he would have enjoyed and excelled in. Would he have enjoyed scholastics, sports, or music? Would he have married and had children? Not being able to know my child is very painful and the emptiness is unexplainable. Also, not having my spouse near to put his arm around me so that we could cry together caused many days of loneliness.

A question I had to learn to endure was when people would ask how many children I had. With the loss of a child, there is no word to describe his or her death as there is with losing a spouse (widow or widower). If I mentioned having two children, the question about each came next within the conversation, and I had to share that Kirk had been killed. Then I had to go into the details of the car wreck and all the other losses in my life. I could always tell that this made the other individual very sorry they had even asked. They never knew how to respond to such an ugly story. To avoid this, sometimes I would just answer one. Then the guilt always grew inside me that I had not recognized Kirk.

I only had thirteen months with Kirk. He was a laid-back, quiet baby with a special smile. I loved to tickle him under his chin just to see that wonderful smile. Also, when I held him, I enjoyed rubbing his left hand and fingers; they had this special softness that I can still feel today.

Fourteen years later, secular singer Eric Clapton wrote the song *Tears in Heaven* as a tribute to his four-year-old son, Conor who had fallen from the fifty-third floor of a skyscraper in New York City in 1990. This has become a special song to me, especially since it was written by someone who lost their child and knows the hurt of such a loss. Every time I hear it on the radio, Kirk comes into my mind and tears swell within me as I wonder if Kirk will recognize and know me in heaven.

> Beyond the door
> There's peace, I'm sure.
> And I know there'll be no more
> Tears in heaven.
> Would you know my name
> If I saw you in heaven?
> Will it be the same
> If I saw you in heaven?
> I must be strong
> And carry on.

With God's help, I will continue to be strong and carry on this journey so that I can see you, Kirk.

Hatred was not part of my life before the wreck. I felt that God had given me a special attribute for discovering something special in everyone. I admit that sometimes I have to dig deep to uncover each individual's uniqueness, but I always discovered it. All this came to a sudden halt in my life the moment the anger started in the hospital after the insurance adjustor explained how the wreck occurred. I developed a hatred that was very heavy and consumed my daily life for ten years—yes, ten years. I developed an unfathomable hatred for a twenty-six-year-old man who I did not know anything about but his name. One thing I did know about this young man, though, was that he had killed my family, leaving me with this unbelievable huge plate of major life events and changes that I am still attempting to cope and live with. In the early days after the wreck, people, both believers and nonbelievers, said to me, "You know where he is today for killing your baby and husband," and I agreed, knowing that is what he deserved. I held onto the belief that he would pay for what he had done to my life.

There is no way God wants us to have this hatred in our life even when someone has completely destroyed us. He started to talk to me through Scripture, revealing how wrong I was. It took a long time and several arguments before I could change this. You see, I thought I deserved to hate this man. But I was judging and determining what I thought was correct, and God showed me that I was completely wrong. Only God has the right to judge. He does not want anyone to miss out on His eternal glory. If a person does, *we should have pity for them, not glory in it.*

But I fought this. After ten years and with God's help, I finally was able to develop a true pity for this young man, even though he had killed my family and himself. I now see that he lost so much too. He never had the opportunity to marry nor have children. At the early age of twenty-six, his life was cut short of the enjoyment here on earth. But I want to make sure that everyone understands: I still have hatred for the alcohol he drank and his getting behind the wheel of an automobile, thinking that he was capable of driving that night. That was the true cause of the wreck. *It is okay to hate the things that are not right, but not people.*

Becoming a single parent during the seventies and eighties and having an only child came with a price and unseen challenges. There was an overwhelming assumption in society that single parenthood and being an only child gives way to bad behavior and a future of uncertainty for the child. Society assumes they go together. I hated those days. I felt like Chad and I were always under a microscope, being watched and criticized. I even had someone telephone me when Chad was in elementary school saying that it was highly possible that Chad might become gay because he was being raised by a single mother. There were times I just wanted to run away as fast as I could with Chad and hide from our culture's atmosphere that surrounded us—one that was not chosen by Chad or me. Countless times, I have wished it could have been different for us, especially for Chad.

I have an endless list of "whys" for God, the biggest being, "Why did Chad and I survive the wreck when the opportunity was there for us to die? Instead, we were both forced to go through these unwanted trials." I always felt it was so unfair that everyone in the family was enjoying heaven while Chad and I were struggling to survive the unpleasant things that were being thrown upon us here on earth. I became very jealous of the family members I had lost.

Every day of my journey, I have been so upset knowing what Chad lacked in his life with the absence of his dad; there were so many opportunities that Gary would have given him that I could not. At times, I found myself yelling out loud to that twenty-six-year-old for drinking and driving, and for robbing my son of so many opportunities and leaving him without a father and a brother to love him. I became bitter watching my son struggle daily with even the little things. I also watched him endure his own emotional pain and thought how different life could have been. How I yearned for that "all-American family" to come back again.

The two years that Chad had with his dad, Gary did so many exciting things with him, including taking him for rides on the tractor, in the combine, and in the "big brown truck" (as Chad called it). It was extremely important to Gary that he have these special times with his boys, as he had enjoyed this closeness with his own dad and wanted his boys to experience the same. There was no way of filling this void in Chad's life. I could only continue to be the mother that God was allowing me to be, give Chad the love he needed, and pray that God would fill the emptiness that had also entered his life.

Psalm 68:5 became my cornerstone for Chad while I raised him, "Father of the fatherless . . . is God." Even though I thought Chad should have his earthly father to guide and love him, it was even greater to realize that God promised to take that place. Since I did not have Gary to share the little daily things that Chad did or be able to talk with him over a concern, I went daily to God for even the littlest things. He promised that He would be the father of the fatherless. In times of desperation, I reminded God of His promise.

I prayed for years that a safe, male friend would be a part of Chad's life. I did not want a forced friend or one who was doing his duty or as a favor for me, but one who would find joy and fun in being with Chad and doing things with him on a regular basis that I could not do. But for some reason this prayer was never answered. Only God knows why.

I am truly thankful for my friends who took the time to include Chad and me in so many activities. These memories are special, including weekend retreats to the beach and Mount Hood, family camp each year, plus many other activities. I have to admit it was hard for me to be around couples and to see families together. I kept my feelings locked inside me because I knew Chad needed to have the opportunity and the experience of being around families—especially the men in the group when he was younger. As time passed and Chad got older, he also began dealing with his own hurt and resentment when around families, which he desired to have. Not having a whole family unit like others became hard for both of us. In order to keep our sanity, we moved into other avenues, deviating from the "norm" of families.

I fought within myself the battle of being single. I hated this singleness after enjoying married life to the fullest. But those married days, with their marvelous enjoyment, had been few and suddenly ended with a boom in a split-second, creating this unwanted, detestable life of singleness. I was just thirty years old, did not want to be a widow, and found the word disgusting and appalling. To find other widows my age was impossible. I spent many hours on the telephone sharing with Mary, who was also dealing with the similar situation of widowhood. Oh, how I wished she could be near instead of eighteen hundred miles away. I did not fit in with the singles that were my age and being with couples was even more of a nightmare. "Being the third wheel" and dealing with so many new situations that you do not even think about when you have a mate. There were numerous stepping stones that a single, who once was married, had to deal with in a group. Even though everyone was wonderful to include me, I missed my other half and wanted him back to be near me and for us to be a couple again. There was no substitute, but I knew that I needed to try finding a new path and some contentment in this single life.

During the Sunday evening service at church, the pastor had us write one thing that we were struggling with and needed God to rally around to help us conquer. Then we were to place our request on the altar, I wrote "accepting single life." From that night of committing this to God at the altar, the load became lighter. My desires would be to have my mate beside me, but thankful for God providing me with many other wonderful avenues, new experiences, and giving me achievements to fill the emptiness of not having my mate. God has promised to go with me into new beginnings. I have not been alone in these pursuits.

I knew that, with God's help, I needed to start building another plate of new challenges, events, and goals for my life. I could not stay buried in the highly piled plate of unwanted events. Even though I am still nibbling away at the "change event" plate created from the wreck as well as other events in my life, I do have another plate with new goals that are constantly expanding. The changes have been hard and have included mistakes and setbacks. But I continue to move forward with a willing heart to learn new meaning in life, which does not have to be with a mate but only with my heavenly Father. The following words from the song *He Knows My Name*, written by Tommy Walker, expresses the love that God has for me:

> I have a Father
> He calls me His own
> He'll never leave me
> No matter where I go.

He knows my name
He knows my every thought
He sees each tear that falls
And He hears me when I call.

We have a choice in our adult life to either stay buried in the events that are handed to us (even though they may be unfair and not our choice) or we can create new goals, with God's help, mark them off as we complete them, and continue on our journey. I did not want to stay buried in that blaming life. The blaming game was unhealthy for me and I wanted to grow. Even though the journey has been very hard and slow, the results from the challenges have been worthwhile. Yes, there are many stones that I have encountered along my new path, where I have stubbed my toe and fell, but I picked myself up from the collapse. At times, the fall hurt, and I just sat with my head buried and cried. But it was important that I continue, so I picked myself up and pushed on.

There is nothing perfect on this earth. The only perfect place will be heaven. If I put my eyes and dependence only upon people, who are human and flawed, for my happiness, it will never come because humans will always fail me. The only happiness and peace I have is found in my relationship with Jesus Christ. There have been so many times in my journey when I wished for something else from individuals that I never received, but Jesus has never failed me in any way. I know that the things that I think are important on earth now will be nothing in heaven.

Our minds are so minute compared to God. We make enormous mountains over something that cannot be changed. If we stay at that point and keep on chewing in it, constantly blaming others even after God has forgiven, forgotten, and changed people, we will never be able to move on to what God has for us. I didn't want to stay in that circumstance forever, so I set goals to keep pressing forward and get out of the "I" attitude.

I cannot imagine what God has in store for me in the days ahead or in heaven. I will always make sure that I keep my relationship with God while here on earth to ensure that I see what glory waits for me later. That eternal home will be a place to live without the tears, heartaches, pain, and harm. I must hang onto that scarred hand of Jesus (yes, Jesus has his physical scars, too) to continue on this journey to the end.

Chapter 8

❧

Throughout my emotional journey, I also had several physical events to deal with. I have learned to live with daily pain in my knee and leg and also have learned how to work around the disability of the knee. The alignment of the leg was not correct when they needed to take me off traction, so going down a slanted slope has always been dreadful and has limited several activities. I have learned to go ahead and do what I can.

I did have another surgery, an arthroscopic, about six years after the wreck. The orthopedic surgeon discovered that beneath the knee cap was mush and had to scrape half of the knee cap away. Plus, he shortened a ligament to help in the slipping of the knee that I was experiencing.

Just a couple years after the wreck, osteoporosis arthritis had already started to set into the knee joint. As the years have passed, additional damage from the arthritis and pain continue to increase, causing the bones in the knee joint to be deformed. The time is getting close for a knee replacement, but until the correct time is scheduled, I will continue to clench my teeth and tolerate the pain. For some reason, I never wanted others to feel my physical burdens too. There are times when the pain is unbearable. I know that Chad, being the closest to me on a daily basis, knows when I am hurting or sees me walking in pain. He has mentioned to me several times that he wished I did not have to suffer and has expressed anger that I have to endure such pain.

I have found walking to be one of the greatest movements I can do for my leg. Also, taking walks has been the best mental therapy I have encountered, giving me time to meditate and just enjoy nature. I took up walking in the nineties. When I was fifty years old, I joined a team to walk in the "Portland to Coast" marathon, which occurs each August in conjunction with the "Hood to Coast" run. I was exhilarated when I crossed the finish line at the beach in Seaside that Saturday morning, knowing that I had made another milestone with my leg and had another personal achievement in my pocket. I have the medal that I received hanging in my bedroom to remind me that, even with the physical and emotional humps in my life, I can succeed by setting my mind in reaching a goal—even if it seems impossible at the time.

As the years passed after the wreck, I was very fortunate to be able to stay at home during my physical healing and be a full-time parent to Chad. I also assumed volunteer activities at church, in my community, and, most of all, at Chad's school and his activities. Being involved in everything that Chad took part in was very important. He needed a parent present. Since I was the only parent, it was very taxing at times (it would have been nice to be able to share these experiences with his father), but I was very grateful for the opportunity to be with Chad during his field trips, sport practices and games, boy scouts, and church activities.

I knew I would need to obtain employment in the future. Since I had not worked for several years, I felt I should get my college degree. So, in the late eighties, I resumed my college studies at Portland State University.

After celebrating Thanksgiving weekend at my home in 1990 with, Mother, Chad, my nephew, Bruce Hellinga, and his wife, Pam, I was working on a paper for school. I was entering the final two weeks of the first term of my senior year, when suddenly I became deathly sick to my stomach. Thinking I was experiencing the first signs of the flu, I continued to work on my paper until I could no longer function. I lay down, thinking that the symptoms would go away, but the pain only got worse. Soon I couldn't maintain my balance when I walked. Finally, I went to bed, but when I needed to go to the bathroom, it was impossible to walk, and I needed to get Chad's assistance. The next morning, I could not get out of bed. Chad, fifteen at the time, asked if he should stay home from school with me, but I felt that I could manage on my own. I knew that I could call my neighbor if I needed help.

I remained in bed until Chad came from school. The symptoms were not subsiding, so I knew that I needed to go to the emergency room. Chad called the neighbor but she was not home, so he carried me downstairs to the garage, placed me in the backseat of the car, and drove me to the hospital with his friend. This would have been fine, but Chad only had a driver's permit and had not yet driven too frequently on the freeway. Considering the circumstances, he did a super job getting me to the emergency room, where I was admitted to the hospital for the night for observation.

No tests were performed to determine what had made me so sick and unable to walk. However, by morning, since I was able to walk on my own, I was released from the hospital.

But the next couple of days at home, I had some unusual signs happening in my body that told me there was still something that was not correct. While trying to slice a piece of meat, I was unable to keep my finger on the knife to guide it. In addition, my writing was just scribbles and barely legible. I could not control my hand and fingers to construct the correct shapes for each letter. And when I turned my head from side to side, it was very difficult to keep my balance. I telephoned the doctor, who insisted that I come in immediately to see him.

After examining me, my doctor immediately sent me to the hospital for a computerized axial tomography (CAT) scan of the brain. When the CAT scan was completed, I knew something was not correct by the nurse's behavior. She even told me "good luck" when I left.

The results of the CAT scan revealed a tumor. In addition, it showed I had a brain hemorrhage in another area, which had caused me to be deathly sick to my stomach a few days earlier. The hemorrhage also had caused a light stoke on my right side, leaving me with the loss of fine motor skills in my right hand and my speech was slightly affected.

Once again, God was watching over me. My not getting the medical treatment that I needed immediately could have resulted in additional effects from the stroke or, even worse, death. I still do not have fine motor control in my right hand for writing and other functions. Also, when I am tired, my speech is affected, but I am thankful that God was protecting me each step at that time.

So, the week before the first term finals, I was finding out that I had this new health issue. With my body not functioning correctly, how could I take my finals? I checked to see if they could be postponed until January. For one of my classes, I had a visiting German professor who would not be returning to the university, and he needed me to take his test before he left. So I decided to take all the finals as scheduled in December. It was extremely challenging to even make it to school; moving my head made me very dizzy, and I could not walk a straight line. Trying to focus on my studies was a great trial. With prayers from friends and family, I did make it through the finals, and was so thankful for Christmas break, which allowed me to regain my strength before starting the winter term.

I had two more terms before graduation in June, and I needed to finish in order to get a job. I was determined to stay on schedule. But how was I going to focus on classes and studying, tackle the new health challenges, and prepare to get a job? I was also dealing with the unknown of the tumor. Only with God's help was I able to concentrate and maneuver another hairpin curve in my journey.

Appointments were made with the neurosurgeon, who ordered a magnetic resonance imaging (MRI) and a cerebral angiography, all of which confirmed the bleed and the tumor. Since the tumor was not in an area where surgery could be performed, the neurosurgeon wanted to wait to see how fast the tumor was growing by scheduling regular MRIs before any treatment.

The results from the next MRI showed that the tumor was slow-growing (which was good news) and treatment could be detained until later. With this news, I was able to continue with the last two terms of college. I proudly graduated on June 7, 1991 (this would have been Gary's and my twenty-third wedding anniversary) with a bachelor of science in economics. Chad, Mother, Peggy, and Roger were in attendance to celebrate this milestone in my life at Portland Memorial Coliseum.

This additional health issue as I was finishing the last two terms of college was certainly not in my plans. I had only enough strength to attend classes and do the necessary homework; I was so exhausted that I could not begin any extra activities in my life. Thankfully, God gave me just enough strength for eight months to complete all the requirements to graduate. I was able to complete another goal that I had set a few years earlier.

PORTLAND STATE UNIVERSITY
Commencement
June 7, 1991

The neurosurgeon ordered another cerebral angiography and MRI in the fall of 1991. It was determined that the best treatment was a radiation treatment that would encircle the tumor to shrink it, but it was still experimental. The only place that did this treatment was at Stanford University Hospital in California. After getting the insurance approval, I was scheduled for the radiation treatment in January 1992.

I decided to work for a temporary service until I had my treatment and knew everything with my health was adequate. My first short assignment was in October, and then in November, I got an assignment in the accounting department at a large technology corporation. This assignment turned into a longer one, with my being hired as a contactor in April, and then permanently hired in November of 1992. God again worked miracles in providing employment when I did not have the strength to look on my own. I worked for the corporation for eighteen years—the last eleven years were as a financial analyst in the company research and development division that creates the new generation of computer chips in Hillsboro—before retiring in the spring of 2010.

In January, Chad, Mother, and Peggy (my wonderful support group) joined me in California for the treatment. We arrived on Friday to relax and did tourist things to keep our minds busy like visiting Alcatraz, Chinatown, The Pier, and driving to Santa Cruz.

On Monday, I entered the hospital where I was taken into an examination room for preparation for the treatment, which included screwing a halo into my head. The day was very long with this heavy contraption on my head. First was another MRI, and then sitting in the room for several hours while the radiation equipment was being prepared with the correct measurements; if they were off by even one hair, the radiation would destroy good brain cells.

When the equipment was finally ready, I was taken into a room with a huge "High Voltage" sign on the door and was placed on a table where they screwed my head down so that there would be no movement. Then they double checked the measurements again. Since the treatment was high voltage radiation, everyone left the room, shutting the door and leaving me alone on the table when the machine was started. After the treatment and the removal of the halo, I was released from the hospital with prescription pain pills. Praise God, the pain pills were never opened. In fact, we went to the shopping center that night, flew back home on Tuesday, and I was back to work on Wednesday.

The MRI a few months later revealed that the tumor had shrunk and that only the scar from the bleed was visible. Praise God again for His healing and for wonderful medical inventions.

PART FOUR

"Usually when people are sad, they don't do anything. They just cry over their condition. But when they get angry, they bring about a change".

—James Russell Lowell

Chapter 9

❧

After the wreck, I was convinced that I needed to share my story. At first, I thought it should be to the Christian community, sharing what God was doing in my life through tragedy.

I also had an inner tugging that I should be influencing our society that drinking and driving is destroying lives. My family should not have died in vain; I, as a survivor, need to keep their story alive. I must persuade others not to drink and drive by sharing what happened in my life. I had the aspiration to do my part in some small way, although I was unsure as to where I should start in letting people realize that drinking and driving is wrong and deadly. But only God knew how this would materialize.

In the early eighties, I noticed a small newspaper article that a woman, whose husband had been killed by a drunk driver, was starting a chapter of Mothers Against Drunk Driving (MADD) in my county. At that moment, I realized God was opening a door to a journey to assist in fighting this immense battle against drinking and driving. I immediately telephoned the woman; from that contact that morning, my long journey in fighting this horrible yet accepted crime in America began.

People's attitudes regarding driving while intoxicated upsets me deeply. Over the years, I have heard so many excuses:

1. I know the road I am driving on.
2. It is just a country road without much traffic.
3. Just a mistake or error. No big deal.

4. I know what I am doing. I have driven many times after drinking and made it.
5. The cost of a taxi would be too much.
6. I will drive slowly.
7. If I call someone to come and get me, they will get upset.
8. There are no issues with my being intoxicated. I can maneuver a motor vehicle in any shape.
9. I had only one drink (when in reality it was several).
10. And the big one: Nothing will ever happen to me.

I have also heard over and over from people that they would never harm or kill anyone. This belief that "it will never happen to me" is still prevalent. But once a person gets behind the wheel of a vehicle after drinking, they become a *potential killer.* That is a strong statement, but very true for everyone; no one is exempt. It does not matter who you are or what your status is. A person may or may not kill, but they become a *potential killer* if they use alcohol or other drugs and *intentionally* get behind the wheel of a vehicle and drive. This is equal to playing Russian roulette. It takes only one bullet to discharge and kill; it takes only one trip around a curve on the wrong side of the road and hit a car and seriously injuring or killing innocent people, including yourself. People need to fully comprehend that driving a vehicle is a privilege that takes one hundred percent clear concentration and attention. It cannot be done with a mind that has been clouded with alcohol or other drugs.

I have thought several times about the twenty-six-year-old man who hit our automobile. If someone had told him an hour before the wreck that he would be killing five people plus himself and critically hurting two other people, what would have been his excuse for still getting behind the wheel intoxicated? Would he have said that he would never harm or kill anyone or that it would never happen to him? But it did happen—to all of us.

In my early days with MADD, I chose to do court monitoring where I sat many hours on hard benches in courtrooms, listening to drunk driving cases, and taking notes as to how attorneys and judges were handling them. I found that some judges took driving under the influence very seriously, but there were others who did not. It became apparent that new laws needed to be created and legislated to remove people from the road who could harm others. I was able to attend when new drunk driving laws were introduced into legislation in the eighties in Oregon's capitol, Salem. I supported the proposed laws and have seen several become law.

Martin Luther King Jr. stated "The ultimate measure of a man is not where he stands in moments of comfort, but where he stands at times of challenge and controversy." I had to move out of my comfort zone to address this controversial issue publicly. This was truly a challenge since I am shy and public speaking is something I always avoided. Also, I never wanted to display my experience or create an "I" attitude. I only wanted to help others in my quiet manner to avoid tragedy in their own lives.

I began speaking along with other victims at high school assemblies and driver education classes where we shared our experiences of how a drunk driver had affected our lives. Talking with the young people was a continual highlight for me. Hopefully what we shared steered their decisions in the correct direction. I looked into their faces and saw so much potential in each one. I always stressed that they not ruin or destroy their potential with alcohol or other drugs by reminding them that they are the future and have a place in our society.

In the late eighties, the courts in Washington County of Oregon added a new program into their system, the Victims Impact Panel. As part of the sentence for those who were driving under the influence of intoxicant (DUII), the judge required them to attend the Victims Impact Panel. Here they heard panelists share how the actions of an intoxicated driver had impacted and changed their lives. When I was asked to serve on the panel, I went to God in prayer, because this was another type of audience. These people had already been convicted, and I wanted to make sure that God would give me the correct attitude for this undertaking. I had an interview, shared my story with the director of the program, and was accepted as a panel member.

God knew that I needed to be with others who had similar experiences and were also hurting from the damages of alcohol-related wrecks. The other people on the panel had experienced or had a loved one that had been affected. From this common thread, we started bonding, which I was unable to get any place else. It was necessary for us to join together for coffee and dessert to unwind from the emotions triggered by the ugly stories that were shared during the panel session. This occasion together also became a time for supporting each other.

Other victims' being Christians was an added blessing. One of the victims was a pastor from a church in Aloha, whose daughter, son-in-law, and two grandsons were killed on Christmas Eve in California by a drunk driver. Their automobile was broadsided by a van without lights and pushed into a tree in a nearby orchard. One of his granddaughters, who was elementary age at that time, had stayed behind with her grandparents in Oregon. Her grandparents had to tell her the next morning that her parents and brothers were dead. What a Christmas present for this young girl! The van driver and his passenger suffered only minor injuries, but he had killed four people and destroyed a family. There are so many heart-wrenching stories, all because of an intoxicated driver.

For twenty years, I served on the Victims Impact Panel, sharing my family's story about ten times a year. This was very draining, and relating how horrible that spilt-second was and the impact it had on my life never became easier. I always arrived a few minutes early and sat in the car praying for strength to share again. But, most of all, I prayed that just one person would hear the truth: How serious it is to drive while intoxicated. This was the only reason I was there, reliving the horrible details of the wreck: to save one life. It was always worthwhile to have people tell me after the session how my story affected them and to hear their promises to get help and not drive while intoxicated.

My practice was to bring Kirk's half-empty baby book to each session. I showed it to the audience and shared that this was what was left of my baby. But behind the scenes, I clung to that book as I walked into the room filled with convicted DUII individuals (each session had around 150 to 200 in attendance). In my mind, I told Kirk this was our time together. I felt like I was accomplishing something with my son even though he was not physically there.

As a part of the program, the audience was to write notes at the end of the presentation. I still have some of them, which I still read and pray that they remember the stories. Here is a note from a high school student:

> Dear Linda, Thank you so much for coming and speaking to us today. I admire your courage. Though you had no choice and were a victim, the way you have dealt with your pain is admirable. You have my deepest sympathies on the loss of your family, especially your beautiful son. I feel strange writing to you, as I am a stranger, but you have connected to me today with your story. I'll never forget you, and I will never ever drive drunk. I wasn't going to anyway, but thank you for the reminder. God Bless. Love Claire

Back in the sixties and seventies, the United States was involved in the Vietnam War. This was very real to me since this was my era, and my peers were involved in this debatable conflict. I remember so well the protesting, flag burning, those fleeing to Canada, the awful pictures on the nightly news and in the newspapers of those killed or wounded, and having a friend come home in a wheelchair, partially paralyzed. The attitude of many Americans toward the soldiers when they came home, even spitting on them, was an extremely sad time for our country. During this war, the draft was implemented, and Gary got his draft papers a year after we were married. I helped pack his small bag and took him to the bus that morning for his ride to Boise for his physical, not knowing if I would see him again that day or not. But I got a telephone call a few hours later; they were sending him back home because his blood pressure was over 200.

I am so thankful for those who serve in our armed forces, protecting each one of us. America lost 58,267 people during this conflict from 1956 through 1975. I can now understand how the families hurt for their children and spouses who were killed. I have visited the Vietnam Wall in Washington, DC twice, and each time, as I touched those names on the wall, tears swelled within me, knowing how each one sacrificed their lives in this conflict. I think of their families and friends and the suffering that they have endured and still endure. But during that same time frame of nineteen years, within the borders and on the soil of the United States, there were around 380,000 people (based on twenty thousand per year, which could be low, but based on 1982 stats) who were killed in alcohol-related wrecks. I'm sad to say, and please do not think I take this lightly, but this is over six times more than those lost in action in Vietnam during the same period of time.

Americans' attitude about drinking and driving was not protested, even with so many deaths. Those deaths were *widely accepted;* no one was spitting on or yelling at the drunk drivers. Finally, there was a small group of people in the late 1970s that saw how many lives were being lost, and laws were beginning to be passed within each state to address this major crime. Since 1980, 2300 anti-drunk-driving laws have been passed within the states, and praise the Lord, the percentage of alcohol-related fatalities is becoming lower each year. I still ache that there are still around 15,000 people killed each year from alcohol-related wrecks within the United States boundaries. To help you picture this, we are losing a small city every year in the United States. There must be continuous education, law enforcement, and any other work that will diminish this crime and save 15,000 lives each year. *The number should be zero. No one should be driving under the influence.* There are other countries with laws in place with zero-blood-alcohol levels to drive a vehicle. The United States needs to follow these countries example to save the 15,000 lives that are lost each year. How sad that the United States cannot be the leader for other countries to follow.

Following is a chart from the National Highway Traffic Safety Administration (fall of 2010), giving the data of those who has lost their lives in alcohol-related fatalities per year from 1982 through 2007. The numbers are overwhelming; these fatalities could have been prevented. In this timeframe, 510,131 were killed in alcohol-related fatalities.

Five hundred thousand deaths in twenty-six years are beyond comprehension—and this is *after* states have adopted harsher driving-under-the-influence laws and cars have become safer. And these numbers do not include those wounded or who have permanent physical injuries caused from alcohol-related incidents. Knowing how many people are suffering from losses similar to mine is heartrending.

	Total fatalities	Alcohol related fatalities	
Year	**Number**	**Number**	**Percent**
1982	43,945	26,173	60
1983	42,589	24,635	58
1984	44,257	24,762	56
1985	43,825	23,167	53
1986	46,087	25,017	54
1987	46,390	24,094	52
1988	47,087	23,833	51
1989	45,582	22,424	49
1990	44,599	22,587	51
1991	41,508	20,159	49
1992	39,250	18,290	47
1993	40,150	17,908	45

1994	40,716	17,308	43
1995	41,817	17,732	42
1996	42,065	17,749	42
1997	42,013	16,711	40
1998	41,501	16,673	40
1999	41,717	16,572	40
2000	41,945	17,380	41
2001	42,196	17,400	41
2002	43,005	17,524	41
2003	42,643	17,013	40
2004	42,518	16,919	39
2005	43,443	16,885	39
2006	42,532	15,829	37
2007	41,059	15,387	37

Data from the National Highway Traffic Safety Administration
http://www.alcoholalert.com/drunk-driving-statistics.html

When violent crimes transpire in a vehicle, they are ignored and perceived by our culture as a normal occurrence. My loved ones' injuries on November 19, 1977, are beyond comprehension. If the same intoxicated twenty-six-year-old man had entered our home and beaten each one, resulting in the same injuries they had received in the vehicle, it would have been a major crime, and the world would have been outraged. But since it happened in a vehicle by an intoxicated individual, our culture persists in ignoring it.

In the wreck, Kirk had taken a blunt force to his head, which caused his death. Gary's death certificate listed the cause of death as a left pneumohemothorax (blood and air in the left lung cavity). I also heard that most of his bones had been broken. The reality is that these horrific injuries resulting in death could have been prevented if someone had not driven while drunk. Vehicle wrecks caused by an intoxicated driver are very violent. We should be outraged and not call them an accident or error. *There is no excuse for driving under the influence!*

PART FIVE

"Hundreds of dewdrops to greet the dawn,
Hundreds of bees in the purple clover,
Hundreds of butterflies on the lawn,
But only one mother the wide world over."

—George Cooper

Chapter 10

❦

A big part of my journey has been with my mother, Goldie Real. I was privileged to help mother as she entered her golden years and needed special care. She gave me so many hours of her time, not only in raising me, but taking care of my physical needs after the wreck without any complaints, and most of all, the hours she spent with Chad. Now it was my turn to give back to her. I need to share how her life was affected by the drunk driver and the wreck beyond taking care of Chad and me.

Mother had an extremely difficult childhood. She did not have a stable home and had to live with different families in several locations in Nebraska, Kansas, and Oklahoma back in the early 1900s. She learned the meaning of work at an early age, and this followed her through many decades until she could no longer do even the most simple tasks because of her physical condition. There was a mixture of events that took place in her childhood that she kept to herself. However, once in a while, she would mention something that had affected her as she was growing up, such as her favorite doll being thrown away. Maybe this doll was her only security at that time.

Mother had grown up in a generation where love was a word in the dictionary but was never verbally related. Even if I did not ever hear the word *love* from her, I still knew I was loved by the numerous things she did for me. After her marriage to my dad on December 31, 1928, her life made a 180-degree turn. My father was a gentle, loving person who embraced my mother. He took her under his arm and, even through their adversities, gave her the stable life that her life up to that point lacked. After their marriage, they settled on a small farm in Nebraska where my brother, Lloyd, joined the household in 1930. Everything proceeded in a positive manner for their first few years of marriage. Then the dust bowl in the thirties hit Nebraska, destroying all their crops and forcing the loss of everything they owned on the farm. They packed up what possessions remained into their 1930 pickup and headed to Wyoming, where they homesteaded outside of Riverton. First, they built a sod house where they lived for a few years until they were able to build a wooden house. From everything I collected, mother worked hard during those days and helped Dad create every block of sod for their house.

My sister, Peggy, joined the family in September 1941. The following November, my brother, who was eleven, was ice-skating with a friend on a pond near the property when he fell through the thin ice and drowned. His death shattered and overtook my mother; in her grief, she was only able to meet three-month-old Peggy's basic needs. After losing Kirk, I understood how my mother always had an empty spot in her heart for the loss of her son. And also like my mother, I too was only able to meet Chad's basic needs for a long period of time due to my grief.

I joined the family in July 1947, five years before my father passed away in 1952 of a heart attack. His death created another void in my mother's life. From losing Gary, I now understand that when your spouse dies, a part of you dies as well. Oh, how I could now relate to my mother. We both had lost a son and mate and shared the emptiness that those losses bring.

After my father passed away, Mother felt strongly that she needed to move away from Wyoming. She had heard about the college in Nampa, Idaho, and decided that would be a great place to relocate and raise her daughters, even though she had never been there. So, the summer of 1954, when I was seven, Mother found someone with a truck to move the furniture, and we left friends and family in Wyoming for Nampa, Idaho, a strange place for the three of us to experience a new beginning.

My mother was truly an amazing and courageous lady to enter this new journey in her life. What a step of faith and dependence upon God she had when making this major move. Above all, she had a special love for her daughters and sought to put us in another environment and give herself a new beginning. What wisdom she had to leave the past as she did and move on in life. She was such an example! What she did at that point in her life has always left an impression upon me that we must move on and not hold onto the past. It is our choice (no one else's) as to what we do, either staying buried in the blaming game or moving on to new paths and journeys. Mother was making those new paths when we moved to Idaho.

She had always worked on the farm, so finding employment in a new town with only farm experience even seemed like a wonderful challenge to her. She finally narrowed her search and found the job she held for twenty years at the state disability hospital in Nampa, showing her overwhelming love for each of the special needs individuals she cared for.

Mother had a special love for her son-in-law, Gary, who was excellent in taking responsibility for the little things that she was unable to manage herself. He became her handyman, and she delighted in having him around. I found a letter that she had written to us where she referred to Gary as "our Gary." Yes Gary was hers, too. Gary loved to tease, and he found Mother especially fun to kid because of her reactions and the ring of laughter it brought to her and everyone around. Looking back, I do not think Mother had much to laugh about for several years. Those times were special to her and gave her years of pleasure since the death of my father and brother. When Gary was killed in the wreck, Mother had lost another son whom she loved.

Mother loved her four grandchildren and took exceptional pleasure in being around Kirk since he was the youngest and because of his special, quiet personality. She had the privilege of being around each grandchild when they arrived home from the hospital after their birth. One of her utmost delights was giving her grandbabies their bath; I almost had to fight with her to be able to finally give Kirk his bath myself! So with Kirk's death, she had lost her first grandchild, which added another loss of a dear family member to her afflictions. With the loss of a special grandchild, no one else could relate to the emptiness my mother felt except another grandma who had lost a grandchild.

After the wreck, everyone, including myself, was so caught up with what was happening with Chad and me, that mother's emotional needs were forgotten. There have been so many times that I wish I could have put my arms around her and tell her that I recognized her pain and just cried with her over each one of our losses.

On Mother's Day a few years after the wreck, Mother surprised me with an extraordinary ring to denote each one of my family members. Gary's and my birthstones are in the center with Chad's and Kirk's birthstones on each side of ours. This ring represents a circle of love from my mother, and I wear it in constant memory of my family. When I look at each stone, knowing what they symbolize, and the gold band, which is a circle of love to me from my mother, I know that Mother understood my pain.

Huge responsibilities were thrown in Mother's direction after the car wreck. Although she was suffering a great deal herself, she took care of Chad and me when we arrived home from Minnesota. This had to be very taxing for her, but I never heard her complain. Once I was able to take care of my own physical needs, she went back to her own home. Her doors were always open, and she was always willing to care for Chad when I needed someone to take care of him, which turned out to be an enjoyment for her to have his presence in her home. Chad and his grandma developed a special bond from these special times together that lasted throughout the years to come.

We all needed some change in our lives after the wreck and traveling became a big outlet for the three of us. I am so delighted that mother could join Chad and me on the majority of our trips, which gave her many memories and the opportunity to visit so many new places that she would not have been able to on her own. Two years after the wreck, we made our first adventure to Florida, which turned out to be one of many to that state. This turned out to be mother's favorite place; she was especially fond of Walt Disney World. Every time we boarded the plane to Oregon from Florida, Mother would sit in her seat and start to cry because she knew she would not be back. This always gave Chad and me a chuckle. But a few months later, we asked her, "Do you want to go to Florida?" We never got a negative answer.

After I went back to work, my weekends were spent taking care of mother's needs: taking her shopping, fixing her hair, and meeting any other requirements and desires she may have. She always fixed Chad and me dinner on Sunday after church, as this was her way of showing her love and appreciation for us.

In the early nineties, Mother began to show moments of mental deterioration. At first, I denied what was happening. Then I became very frustrated that this could be happening. Her state of mind also created problems within her environment. She would misplace or even hide something and then accuse others of stealing. I spent numerous hours for six years going through her belongings to locate a lost or hidden item. With her fears of people stealing from her it was necessary that she be moved several times. Her final apartment was at an assisted living facility in Forest Grove, Oregon.

I was now giving back the countless hours to Mother that she had given Chad and me. I was so grateful that I was near and could take on this responsibility during these years of her life. I never wanted to be a selfish person and set her aside for others to care for. I only wanted to ensure that her quality of life was what she deserved through her aging process. I admit that there were many times when I became very aggravated and did not know how my strength would withstand all the demands that aroused during this time. This was my first time taking care of a beloved elder who was losing her faculties. These new encounters with mother was like bringing a newborn baby home and working through all the surprises that a baby gives. I had heaps of learning to do.

Chad's special love for Grandma continued even through those difficult years. The care he gave her was unreal, even making sure that she was included in everything possible with his assistance. This was truly beyond comprehension for what most people in their twenties undertake. But the moments that were even more extraordinary to me were the telephone calls from Chad, telling me that he picked up his grandma and took her for a ride in the baby blue Mustang, my first car. So pleased to be riding in this car again, she always softly rubbed the horse emblem on the glove compartment. Chad's unselfish and unconditional love for his grandma constantly touched my heart. He loved her for who she was and was always there for her even through the worst days.

But through all Mother's mental issues, she was a fighter. She developed breast cancer at the age of eighty-nine (they do not even track cancer data at that age, calling it part of aging). She had the lump removed on a spring day in 1999 and came home the same day. She had a remarkable recovery for a woman her age with no treatment besides taking a cancer pill. After she turned ninety that same year in August, we celebrated her birthday in Hawaii as a family.

A couple of years later, Mother started having some unusual pain in her wrist. A bone scan revealed that bone cancer throughout her body. For the next four years, before her death at ninety-six, she lived with the bone cancer. Her complaints of pain were so limited that you would never think that she had this ugly disease. She had also developed diabetes, which is not uncommon at that age. However, she was unable to get it under control with diet and medicine, which created several other complications.

It was difficult to see my mother advancing into this stage of her life. Each day that passed, there were continuing problems that required attention. She lost her appetite, and I visited her about everyday and tried hand-feeding her to give her as much nutrition as I could. Sometimes when I stopped by after work, her caretakers already had her in bed, and she would be sleeping. I would lie down beside her just to be near her and hold her aging, brown-spotted hand, which now felt so soft, just about like baby skin. Holding and rubbing this hand brought back memories of the roughness that these hands once held; roughness caused from the many years of the hard work she had performed in service of others. She was such an unselfish lady who had gone through so many trials and hurts. My mother gave to others through her hands, showing her love. She demonstrated that everything must come from the heart. All else in life is just stuff.

Helen Keller wrote, "The best and most beautiful things in life cannot be seen or even touched. They must be felt with the heart." Yes, it is Mother's love from her heart that both Chad and I have felt deeply in our lives. This is the most beautiful gift and will always be cherished deeply.

Mother's resources were always limited, but she made sure all my necessities were met. I never felt cheated in any way and was thankful that I was her daughter. I was especially thankful for her marriage to my father, who I only had for five years. I remember him as a gentle, loving father with whom I wish I could have shared more years. I also wish that we could have been a complete family with my brother.

After a brief hospital stay in mid-February of 2006 for her elevated diabetes, Mother was able to return to her apartment with the assistance of hospice. She passed away one week later on February twenty-fourth.

Mother had a gravesite in Wyoming next to my father, but she had said many times that she did not want to be buried in Wyoming. I went to the cemetery where Gary and Kirk were buried to see if I could find a spot for Mother near them. As the owner of the cemetery and I walked to Gary and Kirk's gravesite, I looked down at the spot that I had purchased for myself next to theirs and was shocked to find a stranger buried in my spot. The lady was buried a few months earlier next to her husband, who was on one side and, of course, Gary and Kirk were on her other side.

Alarmed, I brought the error to the cemetery owner's attention. We went to the office, examined the books, and found my name marked out on the lot that I had purchased. After much searching for the deed, I finally located it in my safe deposit box. I showed it to the cemetery owner, verifying my purchase of the lot. As a result, the cemetery owner found five spots together and agreed to have Gary and Kirk moved. This was an added stress while making the final arrangements for my mother, but looking back on the error, God was moving everything around for a purpose. He even has control over gravesites.

We made arrangements for three of the five spots available. When Chad heard that his father and brother were going to be moved, he was very upset because this was their final resting spot and thought the lady in my spot should be moved. He was comforted after I explained everything to him and he realized that now his grandmother would be next to his dad and brother.

Since there were five spots available together, I thought I would give Chad an opportunity to purchase one, but he declined. I did not think much about his decision since he was still young and would probably want a spot with his own family if he married. I have to admit that this was a blessing for me in having mother put to rest with her family who she loved so dearly. As a result of the error, the spot next to Mother would be mine, and Gary and Kirk would be moved next to mine the following summer.

A few days after Mother's death, Chad asked if we could have a brick etched with her name placed in the sidewalk at the entrance of Walt Disney World Magic Kingdom. As this had been one of her favorite places, I thought this sounded like an excellent idea. This would be a special memory that her family could enjoy when they visited Walt Disney World. I promised that I would pursue it.

PART SIX

"Son, you outgrew my lap,
but never my heart."

—Author Unknown

Chapter 11

❧

Chad had a very difficult time with the loss of his family. Most people would think a two year old would not have the emotional journey an adult does, but Chad entered the world after the wreck with a darkness that, as the years passed, he internalized. His life events were also piled high with major changes and caused his life to go off course with the losses of his father, brother, grandpa, grandma, and uncle.

As he entered into his third year of life, the routine that he had experienced a few months earlier was now gone. He now had no dad, no brother, and a mother who was entangled in her own emotional suffering and dealing with her physical limitations. During this time frame, only his basic needs could be met by his mother and grandma. None of the fun things he had experienced a few months earlier now existed.

Chad was beginning to show brotherly love toward Kirk and was having those special enjoyable moments that only could exist at their young ages. The picture is still in my memory of watching him and Kirk holding hands and walking through the backyard together just a few days before the wreck. They were becoming friends. How slowly the thirteen months had been for Chad to develop a brotherly bond with baby Kirk: Then how quickly that brotherly bond was stolen from him.

When Chad was around five, we were watching "The Carol Burnett Show." I got so tickled over a scene with Carol and Harvey Korman and started to laugh heartily. Then I noticed Chad, who was seated on the couch across the room from me, staring at me with a peculiar gaze on his face. I realized at that moment that he had not seen me laugh in this manner since the wreck. The sounds of laughter that had filled each room in our house before the wreck had disappeared, leaving only a sullen, quiet atmosphere. Chad was not only stunned but surprised to hear his mom laugh so intensely.

When he entered the first grade, it became extremely apparent that he was starting to experience further emptiness from not having a family like his peers had. Thanksgiving that first year of elementary school, four years after the wreck, was the first time I saw the anger that had built up inside of him about not having his family. We were having Thanksgiving dinner at my mother's. When I parked the car in front of her place, Chad, who was seated in the backseat, out of the blue yelled, "I hate my dad!" This explosion of hate was a bombshell. He did not know this dad he was yelling hatred toward. I was stunned and tears filled my eyes. Once we were out of the car, I put my arm around him and just hugged him, knowing there were no words that could remove that hatred. There are steps a person goes through in grieving, even small children, and one of those steps is anger and hatred.

Chad internalized his emotional wounds. He always shared everything—at times you could not get him to be quiet—but never would he share anything about his father, brother, or the wreck. He would just clam up when the subject was brought up. Although he enjoyed hearing stories about his family, he never wanted to talk about them. As time went on, whenever the topic came up, he would just relate in an angry manner, "If there is a loving God, He would not have allowed the car wreck to happen," and then quickly drop the subject and move on to something else. He not only hated not having his father, brother, grandparents, and uncle, he was also developing a hatred for God and wondered if there even was a God. This wreck created a big emptiness within him that only God could understand.

As Chad entered his teens, his confidence level started to plummet. He forever seemed like he was lost and could never find his niche, which I know is common in teens. He tried every sport that was offered in elementary school, but soon felt that athletics was not his thing. Or maybe it was just harder for him to develop without a man in his life to guide him.

He started to play the alto saxophone in the fifth grade and really connected with music. He developed a connection with the music director who assisted Chad's development on the saxophone and his enthusiasm for music throughout high school, progressing from the alto to tenor and finishing his senior year with the baritone saxophone. His CD collections continued to grow. He also enjoyed going to live performances of some of his favorite groups. Plus, he had so much fun testing my knowledge of songs and artists that were playing on the radio. He knew them all, and I only knew a few.

Once Chad graduated from high school in 1993, he entered a very dark world. I even debated writing about this, but I must, because God had to carry me through this revolting period that Chad had chosen, which included drugs and getting involved with some untrustworthy people. During this time, I took my daily Bible readings and wrote each verse in first person to relate only to me.

I could only relate to God about what was assaulting my life. Of course I clung to the verse that He had given me earlier in Chad's life where He promised to be Chad's father. Those intimate times alone with God, along with writing in my journal, gave me the strength to make it through each day with Chad. God's wisdom about how to handle the circumstances sustained both of us. Chad had made a poor decision on a car he owned and the car was stolen from our property. A few days later, a car load of individuals who had stolen Chad's car showed up in angry late one night. They were upset they could not get a lost-of-title from the Motor of Vehicle office because I had informed the office of the circumstances. I had Chad in his fearfulness, hide. God gave me the words and calmness to converse through the window of the sliding door in my terror. God's protection was with us that night. In a matter of a few days the car was returned.

It would have been so much easier to kick him out of the house and close the door and my eyes to everything that was happening around us, and I knew there were several people who thought the same. Many thought that my allowing him to stay was enabling him. But I am so glad that I listened only to God and not to people who wanted me to take the easy way out (Just a side note: If you are ever in this or a similar situation, pray, and let God do the directing. You can ask for advice from others, but let God give the final word. This is where you will find victory).

The night came that I was ready to tell Chad he had to leave. I laid in bed, asking God to guide me during this time. He responded so clearly, "No. Do not let him leave. This home is Chad's only safe haven, and he must stay here." But I continued to argue with God, thinking only of myself and how I could not go through anymore of the events that were going on in Chad's life and encircling me. Still, God answered me with a compelling, "No."

I reflect back on that night and am so grateful I listened only to God instead of human voices. He knew Chad's needs far greater than I did and gave me the strength I needed to walk with Chad to better days. If I had not listened to God that night and only thought of myself, I would have missed out on the countless blessings that took place within Chad in the months ahead.

On Father's Day when Chad was twenty, he asked if I had gone to the cemetery that day. I looked at him with a puzzled expression, thinking *Why I would go to the cemetery today?* He told me that he did, but did not say any more. I could tell from his voice and facial expression that this had been special for him. I do not know what happened that day in the cemetery or even why he visited his dad and brother's grave, as he had not done so in fifteen years. But, praise God, I felt that Chad was starting to heal after eighteen years from suffering from his huge loss.

During this time frame, the brother of Chad's friend, who was just a year younger and had hung around with them while they were in school, took his own life. This was a heavy burden for Chad, who felt guilty because he had not been a part of this boy's life in the last couple of years. Chad felt in some ways responsible for not helping him through what he was going through. I found the following written in one of Chad's notebooks of poems and thoughts:

Life

Death has its place in time.
Speeding this time to the present only causes sorrow and pain
to us all. A break in nature was never intended to be.

Hope you see this (his friend's name)

Six months later, one of Chad's former girlfriends, who he had not seen in several months, telephoned. Chad was not home, so I chatted with her for a few minutes. I noticed that she did not have that bubbly voice that I remembered when I had spoken to her earlier, and she was saying some out of the ordinary things of Chad's and my past that didn't make sense. When Chad came home, I told him that she had called earlier and wanted him to telephone her back, but he never did. The following week, she took her life. This weighed heavily on Chad. He found it so hard to understand and carried such guilt for not returning her telephone call.

Chad went into seclusion for nearly two years after his friends' deaths and had little contact with anyone other than maybe visiting a friend on Saturday night. He also withdrew into himself, adding more to his grief. He would only share that he did not sleep well because of thoughts of his friends.

The day finally came when Chad was able to move on. He started classes at the community college and received his Aviation Maintenance certificate with excellent grades and completing the Federal Aviation Administration tests, also with high marks. Finally, he received his aviation mechanic license from the US Department of Transportation that he always wanted. He was looking forward to using his skills and education and fulfilling his dream of working on airplanes. But then 9/11 took place, and the aviation field came to an abrupt stop. Even though Chad was disappointed that there were no openings, this did not stop him. He went back to the community college and worked on another certificate along with his associate degree. He was enjoying learning, which became his favorite form of entertainment. His favorite television stations were the Discovery and History channels.

Also during this period, Chad got extremely interested in politics and registered and voted for the first time. Even though we did not always agree on several issues, he made me think outside the box, which forced me to do more research and to listen to both sides of the issues before making any decisions. He was a big supporter of the environment—he was always concerned that nature would be ruined by humans.

Chad enjoyed writing. During his younger years, his writings were pretty abstract. You needed to read between the lines, especially with his poetry, to completely comprehend the message that he was conveying. As he got older, his personal writings and short stories for school always had the theme of a car wreck or a family. Here is one story that expresses his feelings of the car wreck and of death:

Dealing with Death

The first experience a person has with death is often filled with confusion and sorrow. My personal experience dealing with death has been a haunting reality my entire life. I was involved in a tragic car accident when I was very young, which was caused by a hopeless drunk driver. The date was November 19, 1977, and my family had just arrived in Minneapolis, Minnesota, to spend the holiday with relatives. As we drove back from the airport, the accident occurred. Five members of my family were killed instantly, including my father, brother, and grandparents. For reasons unknown, my mother and I were spared our lives from this horrid accident. Growing up, being a survivor of a tragic event, builds a large tolerance toward the sorrow and confusion of death. At the age of twenty-two, I experienced death with a firsthand account when I discovered a close friend of mine, hanging from a tree. When having to deal with losing a close friend in such a manner, it is hard to describe in words what is felt. Death is tough to deal with, but when you grow up living with it, your soul tends to harden up . . ."

Even though Chad was only two when his family members were killed, his losses created a lifelong journey of emotional scars that never left him.

Chapter 12

❧

In September 2004, Chad and I traveled to Yellowstone and the marvelous Tetons in Wyoming. We stayed a few days at my sister Peggy's in Idaho, where we attended a Boise State Broncos football game. They were playing our favorite team, the Oregon State Beavers; sadly, the Beavers lost.

After we returned home a few days later, I received a telephone call while at work from Chad. He had fallen while out on his daily walk with his boxer, Mandy, and his back and leg were hurting. He also said that he apparently had bitten his tongue when he fell because it was swollen. He went on to tell me that someone had called the paramedics when he fell. The paramedics reached him as he was walking back down the hill to our house and told him they were called because he was having a seizure. This shocked Chad and he did not believe what the paramedics were saying about the seizure. He refused any treatment and walked home. I was in disbelief and unable to comprehend what he was saying over the telephone.

After I got home from work that evening, I knew by looking at Chad that he should have had medical attention for his back and leg. His tongue was swollen about half an inch and was black and blue. He finally agreed, and we went to the closest, small emergency hospital in Forest Grove, Oregon.

A small boy in the waiting room asked Chad what he was there for. Chad, who enjoyed making children laugh, just laughed and told him he had fallen and let the boy see his swollen, black-and-blue tongue, which alarmed the boy. We all had a laugh, including the small boy. Children were drawn to Chad and loved chatting with him. They called him "Big Red" because of his short, red beard, six-foot-tall frame, hearty laugh, and wonderful smile.

Chad alongside a falls in Norway, September 2005

After Chad was taken into the examining room, the waiting grew very long. Other patients were going in and coming back out, and I was wondering why it was taking Chad so long. After waiting for over an hour, I heard a huge crash come from the examining room. My heart jumped, wondering what it was and if everything was okay. I kept looking at my watch, but the hands moved so slowly. About an hour after hearing the crash I was summoned back to the examining room. Chad had had another massive seizure while standing and had fallen against some equipment, knocking it to the floor. That explained the crashing noise I had heard while in the waiting room.

The nurse asked me if Chad had had a head injury. I told her that he had a massive one in a car wreck when he was two, but nothing recently. I could tell by her eyes and another nurse's, who was standing nearby, that this concerned them. The ER doctor was sending Chad by ambulance to their sister hospital in Hillsboro, Tuality Hospital, to be admitted in the progressive care unit (PCU). Chad was very unhappy to hear the prognosis of a seizure and was denying and in disbelief about having had another one. He thought the medical team had caused it by the test they ran earlier in the ER. After I confirmed everything with him, he consented to being admitted to Tuality for further observation.

As I sat with him in the PCU at Tuality that night, Chad became extremely concerned that he had no health insurance, and paying for any hospital expenses and treatment was impossible. He was more concerned about this than pursuing the cause of the seizures and receiving the treatment he needed. I could relate to his concerns because Gary and I did not have health insurance the nine-and-a-half years we were married because of Gary's high blood pressure, which was a pre-existing condition. Every time any medical treatment at the hospital was necessary, including the birth of our children, we needed to budget and hope that it would not drain our resources. I used to joke with Gary that if any major medical need occurred, it had better happen in the car, since that was the only medical coverage we had. Oh, what a sad joke that was in reality. The one thing different between Gary and Chad was that Gary was employed, but Chad was not.

The next morning, Chad saw the assigned doctor and was moved to a standard room where a neurologist also examined him, gave him an EKG and prescribed medicine for the seizures. The neurologist wanted to do an MRI, but Chad refused, knowing how much it would cost.

The following day, Chad came home with his medicine but no answers as to what was causing the seizures. The first doctor that Chad had seen in PCU requested that he visit his office for a follow-up. I encouraged Chad to pursue it. Chad made the appointment and went to the doctor's office. Later that day, I got a telephone call at work from Chad, who was so upset because, when he checked in, they asked him for insurance information, and when he told them he did not have any, they refused to let him see the doctor. Chad was so humiliated because everyone in the waiting room could hear what was going on.

My heart ached for him, knowing that he needed health care, but he could not get any medical treatment. I prayed daily that he would have no more seizures in the future. He had enough seizure medication for the next three months. Without the proper monitoring, I wondered what would transpire during and after that time.

Doors opened for Chad. He found employment in November—a contract job as a technician in a Fab that makes computer chips at the large technology company where I worked. Now he was able to get medical insurance. I will always remember hearing Chad say over and over after his experience that there are so many people who need medical help but cannot get the proper treatment without insurance. He thought it was extremely unfair.

After obtaining insurance, Chad was able to get the medicine he needed, have a neurologist monitor his progress, and get the proper tests. The major blessing was that the medicine was what his body needed to protect him from having any more seizures.

August 2005, ten months since Chad's first seizure, I went into the office on a Saturday to complete a complex finance forecast for the next year that was due the following week. Working alone in my small cubicle without any distractions and able to focus on the numbers was good. As Chad was leaving for work that morning (he worked a compress week, twelve hour shift rotating on a three or four day week), I mentioned to him that I was working at the office for a few hours that day. As I was enjoying the quietness, someone entered my cubicle. It was one of Chad's co-workers, informing me that Chad had had a seizure in the Fab and was taken to the emergency room at St Vincent Hospital in Portland. I just sank in my chair.

As I drove to the hospital, the question that constantly kept going through my mind was, "Why, oh, why, was this occurring again in Chad's life?" He had gotten his life back on track, met all his goals in getting his education, and had a job he was really enjoying. These seizures did not make sense. Why were they now interrupting his life? When I arrived in the emergency room, the nurse stated that Chad had had another seizure after he arrived at the hospital. He went back to his neurologist in the next few days where additional tests were performed including a MRI. The tests gave no conclusions on the cause of his seizures. The doctor continued him on the medicine.

Chad had a great desire to visit Norway, to see where his great-grandparents on his father's side of family had lived and to walk on the same ground as they did. Since he had lacked the Sundve's physical presence, he wanted to fill some of the void in other ways. In the middle of September, we were off to Norway for ten days, anticipating the beauty of the country and visiting the Sundve farm which is now at the bottom of a ski lift. After a long, overnight flight, we arrived in Oslo. Our bodies were tired, but we managed to tour the city that afternoon and began absorbing some of the Norwegian culture and sights.

The next morning, we were scheduled to fly north from Oslo, but while acquiring our breakfast from the buffet at the hotel, Chad came back to the table with his food and said he did not feel good. He felt a seizure coming on. As soon as he sat down, I saw his mouth start to quiver and then he went into a full seizure. Quickly, I went to his side to catch him before he fell and alerted the waitress, who assisted me in getting him safely to the floor where he had another massive seizure. They called the paramedics, who took us by ambulance to a local emergency room. They located a French doctor who could speak English to monitor him. This doctor found a neurologist who would be able to see Chad at their main hospital that day, but Chad felt he could wait to see his doctor back in the States since he had an appointment scheduled a few days after he would returned.

We took the taxi back to our hotel, where Chad rested the remaining part of day, and felt well enough to take a walk around the area and through a local park that evening. (As a side note, the Norwegian medical system was amazing in taking care of a foreign individual. Also, the assistance we received in cancelling reservations since we had missed the airplane flight to the north that morning where we had hotel reservation for the next two nights and were now in need of making new travel arrangements were wonderful. We were blessed to be in Norway!)

We left the next day in a rental car with our changed itinerary to immerse ourselves in the beauty of Norway, including a journey down one of the famous fjords. Even after having to modify our travel plans, we were able to find the old Sundve farm and were able to walk in the area of Chad's ancestors.

After returning to Oregon, Chad continued to take medical tests, without any results. At the same time, his employment contract was coming to an end at the high-tech company, so he had applied for a permanent position there. Another high-tech company wanted to hire him after an interview. Adding to his job complexities, an airline company that he had applied to years earlier called with an opening and was interested in hiring him. Then a helicopter company called. He was so overwhelmed after many years of hopeless job searching. He knew that with the seizures he would not be able to accept the job offers from the airline or the helicopter companies, so he decided to remain in the position that he had contracted with and was enjoying over the past year.

In early December, I was awakened by loud cries, and for a few seconds, I thought I was dreaming. Finally, I realized the crying was coming from Chad's room, which was at the other end of the house. I ran downstairs to his room and found him coming out of another seizure. During this one, he had pulled his shoulder out of the socket, which created enormous pain and caused the anguished cries. The doctor tried unsuccessfully to put it back into the socket in the emergency room. They ended up taking him into surgery to position. These seizures were becoming increasingly violent.

I found the following short story in Chad's writings about a young lady we saw have a seizure in 2003 when we were in Iceland at the bus station. Chad was so concerned. I have thought countless times about this incident, particularly once Chad started having seizures:

Disappointment in My Actions

> During a trip to Iceland, I was strolling down the small, picturesque streets of Reykjavik, admiring the sights and sounds of Scandinavia. As I was waiting for the number 5 bus to go uptown, I noticed a little girl lying in a cold mud puddle having a seizure. Having gone through first aid training, I should have jumped into action, but instead I just stood there like a wasteful bystander. The longer I stood there, the more I wondered why I was not doing a thing. A large group of Icelanders began to gawk and stare, but no one did anything . . . After leaving the situation, I was quite shook up and disappointed with myself. I could have proved that I was different in character, but it showed how typically human I truly am.

Chad wanted to visit his lifelong friend, Dale Willis, who now lives in Ketchikan, Alaska, during his four days off the second week in March 2006. Going through the previous months with his aging grandma, her death, and his own heath issues, he needed time with his friend. He left on a flight from Portland International Airport to Ketchikan with both a camcorder and a still camera. He ventured through the mountains around Ketchikan, absorbing the beauty, capturing more nature pictures, and, most of all, just being with Dale.

Chapter 13

❧

Just three weeks and two days since Chad's grandmother had passed away and four days since he had returned from Alaska. On Saturday, March 18, Chad came home for lunch from work. Sensing that another seizure was coming on, he felt that he should not drive or even go back to work. He made the telephone call to his manager, explaining that he was ill and giving him the status of the equipment he was in charge of for his substitute.

Although I felt anxious about leaving Chad that evening, I went to a party at a friend's house. However, once I arrived, I gave Chad a quick telephone call to make sure that everything was still all right. I did not want to stay too late at the party with Chad's condition heavy on my mind, so I left early, arriving home about 10:00. Chad was sitting in the recliner in the living room and was upset with himself that he had not returned to work because nothing more had taken place in his body. I talked with him in the living room, and then I was off to bed, telling him goodnight. He looked at me and said, "I love you, Mom. Goodnight." I turned to him and said, "I love you too. Goodnight." After retreating to my bedroom, I heard him go downstairs to his room.

Sunday, March 19. Chad was usually up by seven, but he never came out of his bedroom before I left for church that morning. I remember thinking while I was having breakfast that the house had an unusually eerie spirit of quiet. I wished Chad was up and kept looking down the hall to his bedroom, hoping to hear some noise, but I knew he had probably had a seizure after he went to bed and needed the extra rest. Seizures always left him extremely exhausted. In the back of my mind, I thought it was strange that he wasn't up yet since he was up before seven, even on his days off. Since I was not going to be home for Sunday dinner, I took time that morning to prepare one of Chad's favorite dishes, which I left on the stove so that he could warm it up when he arose.

After church, I attended a fiftieth anniversary celebration that was being held for friends. I tried to telephone Chad on my cell but got no answer, which left a very uncomfortable feeling in my stomach. I had this suspicion that something was wrong and that I needed to get home, so I left the anniversary celebration early. On the drive home, several things entered my mind. Why could I not reach Chad by telephone? I thought that he probably went to his friends Client and Liz's house, but when I drove into the driveway and saw his Jeep, I became more alarmed.

Entering the quiet house, I noticed that Chad's bedroom door was still closed. I frantically ran down the hallway and knocked on the door. No noise came from the other side. I quickly opened the door; there he was, lying so quietly with one arm under his head, his body partially covered by the comforter with his legs uncovered. I moved over to his body and laid my hands on his arm and leg. I felt no life.

I started screaming and ran from room to room. My mind could not function. What was happening? What should I do? I opened the back door and stood on the patio, wailing. I went back into the house. In my confused state, I grabbed the phone book, trying to look for an emergency number, but could not find one. So I dialed my sister's cell number and my brother-in-law, Roger, answered. He could not understand any of my frantic words. Since they were in a store shopping, he said he would have Peggy phone me back, which she did right away. Finally, she was able to grasp a few words that I was trying to say and told me to call 911. (As I look back on it today, the telephone number 911 had not even entered my frantic mind.)

After calling 911, the female operator asked the normal questions like name and address and also wanted to know if I had tried giving Chad cardiopulmonary resuscitation (CPR). I had to assure her that Chad was dead. She also heard our dog, Mandy, in the background and instructed me to put her in a closed room before the paramedics arrived, which I did. I stood at the front window with the telephone and the operator on the other end, watching helplessly for someone to arrive and give assistance. Once I saw the ambulance coming down the road, there was a sense of relief that filled my body that I was not going to be alone in this state of shock after finding my son dead. The operator stayed on the telephone with me until the paramedics entered the house.

In just a few minutes, my house immediately became full of strangers: the paramedics, men from the local fire department, the county sheriff, state policemen, and the medical examiner. I sat in my chair in the dining room in shock with a medic taking my pulse, which was racing wildly, and administering oxygen to me for a few minutes.

Two of my friends, Joleen Middleton and Rich Dimick, arrived to be with me after receiving the news from my sister. Later, my pastor, Reverend Kevin Donley, and another friend, Jim Powell, joined and prayed with us. Joleen and Rich stayed into the evening until my niece, Barbara Hedrick, arrived from southern Oregon and my sister from Idaho, letting me sit in my quiet shock, trying to comprehend what had taken place that day.

The medical examiner knelt down next to me, stating that he had determined that Chad had passed away around 2:30 a.m. Then he asked a few questions about his medicine and anything else that I know that would have affected his death. The only thing that came to mind, if the Nyquil he had taken for his cold would have any effect on the seizure, the answer was no. Also, he asked if I would like an autopsy performed on Chad, and I instantly said yes. Someone near me said, "I do not think you should." But, at that moment, I needed to discover what had ended his life. I needed answers. Over the last eighteen months, his seizures were extremely worrisome to me, and every one of the tests performed, including the MRI, revealed nothing. The thought of his head injury at age two never escaped me. Now, this final seizure that he had in his sleep had ended his life. I needed to pursue any avenues available for answers. I asked the medical examiner to perform an autopsy to help resolve this mystery.

Chapter 14

❧

The next few days after Chad's death, I went through the motions of existence. My sister and my niece walked beside me to move me through each day, circumstance, and the events during the week. Words cannot explain the difficulty and pain of having already buried one son and now having the task of burying another, and my last, child. When a child dies, the loss creates an unbearable, indescribable hole within a mother. I had to lay my second child to rest in a few days. How much can a mother endure? We expect our children to outlive us!

Notifying friends and family of this yet another tragic event was not easy. My family had been here just three weeks before for Mother's memorial and now were returning for Chad's. What a drain for everyone. One of Chad's friends, Jared, had telephoned the morning after Chad passed asking for him, and I had to tell him that Chad had passed away the day before. I can still hear him breaking up from the staggering news. He was unable to utter a word. Everyone was facing this unbelievable news that Chad had disappeared from our lives so quickly and without any warning. Another sudden death now challenged us all.

My dear Sundve family and Cliff drove from Minnesota for the memorial service to give me their loving support. God has blessed me with such a loving family and friends, plus Chad's wonderful friends, who also surrounded me with their care and tenderness. Hurting people need each other, and God brought us together. Chad's devoted friend for so many years, Dale, from Alaska returned to Oregon for his final good-bye to Chad. This was extremely hard on him; they had been neighbors and friends since elementary school. It was tremendous that Chad was able to make the trip to Alaska to spend a couple of days with Dale earlier in the week. Only God knew that they needed this last, special time together.

Back I went to the cemetery, where we had just buried Mother, to request another spot. What a surprise for the owner. Three weeks earlier, the error that the cemetery had made was very frustrating, but now it was a huge blessing. Chad could be buried with his family, which included part of a family that he did not know but desired so much to have. I gave up my spot again, but this time to a very special person. Chad could have his grandma on one side and his dad and brother on the other. I then purchased another site for me on the other side of Gary and Kirk.

I knew Chad would not want to have a traditional service. I tried hard to meet both of our needs, but I probably met more of my desires. I rode to the church service with my brother-in-law and sister, holding one of Chad's prize bonsai plants (one of his favorite hobbies) on my lap to put next to his casket. While riding in that backseat, I was being nudged that I needed to greet everyone as they arrived instead of being enclosed in a waiting room. I fought with this thought and knew I could not do this on my own. I prayed before leaving the car that God would give me the strength if this was what I was supposed to do. As I was walking into the church, I thought it would be much easier to run and hide, but I felt this need for the hugs from friends. God knew that I needed them, too. It was beyond words how comforting each hug felt that day. I was glad that I listened once again to the nudge within me.

Saying my last final good-bye to Chad was extremely hard. Before his casket was closed, I rubbed the reddish hair on his arm, kissed his forehead, thanked him for being my son, and told him how much I loved and would miss him.

I chose the poem "I Am Free" for Chad's memorial pamphlet. Even though this is a very common poem, I realized how suitable it was to Chad's life. Chad is now free of those awful massive seizures that he had developed the last eighteen months of his life. He is now free from the inner pain of not having his dad, brother, grandparents, uncle, and friends; pain that had forever haunted him. And he is now free from not having fulfilled his dreams of having the wife and children that he desired and of working on airplanes because of the seizures.

Following is the chorus from "I Am Free," written by Jon Egan. Whenever I hear or sing it, Chad instantly comes into my thoughts:

Darkness will flee
My heart screams I am free
I am free to run
I am free to dance
I am free to live for you
I am free

It has been extremely rough on me as a mother dealing with the uncertainty of the final eternal home of their child. I have struggled with this profoundly. My pastor told me not to go down this road that, Chad and God could have met even that night before his death. When Chad was going through his extremely dark years, he avoided even talking about God and debated that God did not exist. In his younger years, he repeatedly said that if there was a God, He would not have allowed the car wreck, leaving him without a father and a brother. This was difficult because I also questioned God, "Why?" And watching Chad suffer so deeply with this issue made my "whys" even greater.

During those hard years, God reminded me that Chad was His and that He would take care of him; Chad was only on loan to me from Him. I finally released Chad to God and stopped preaching to him, but I never stopped praying for him. I know God can even speak to a person in their sleep. Every so often, I asked Chad about his relationship with God, and, as time went on, I sensed that he was growing spiritually. There was no more arguing about God's existence. Then one day about two years before his death, I was urged to ask again. Chad told me, "You would be surprised," and I knew that he had made a commitment. I was shocked and went away praising God. I also noticed that Chad watched some religious programs on television, and he mentioned that he wanted to find a church sometime. I really saw a change in Chad, and I have to remind myself that it is no one's job to judge. Only God will do that—only God knew Chad's heart and past. "He executes justice for the fatherless and widows" (Deuteronomy 10:18).

Trips were very important to Chad and me. During these times, we escaped the tension and anxiety that we encountered in our daily lives. The memories I now have of each trip are priceless. Traveling with Chad was always an excellent experience, but especially in the last few years as good friends instead of as mom and son. We had developed such a wonderful friendship in the last six years of his life. When Chad died, I not only lost my son, I lost my best friend. He was so adventurous and had his own astonishing bucket list of important "must sees." Sometimes I wondered why he wanted to see certain things, but usually these "must sees" became the most memorable part of the trip. Chad had a talent for finding the most extraordinary locations. Also, he always researched the Hard Rock Cafes that might be in the area, as his goal was to visit as many as he could and have his photo taken in front of each one. At the time of his death, he already had twenty-five under his belt.

Our spur-of-the-moment activities during our travels were exciting. We always had our general itinerary of "must sees", but both of us were happy to venture off the main road to look for unusual yet highly photographic settings, such as a special building, a house, a fence, or other picturesque points to capture. Since Chad's hobby was photography, which is one of my hobbies too, we had something in common when traveling. Chad often left the house with the camcorder in one hand and the still camera in the other. He could relax during those times and usually took his dog and maybe a friend to different places to capture unique and, most of all, natural sights, which were his passion. These photos included the beauty of the mountains, lakes, rivers, the ocean, and animals. Through them, you could see that Chad had an exceptional eye.

In my last Mother's Day card from Chad in 2005, he wrote the following:

Happy Mother's Day,
Thanks for the travel, the fun, and the joy. Mom, you're the
best, no one can even get closer. Stay strong and happy.
Love Chad

Chad knew my weaknesses and reminded me once again to be strong. He knew I was overwhelmed by another huge load at that time with my mother ailing and needing so much in-depth care, deadlines at work, and, of course, my concerns for Chad's physical issues.

With Chad's death, additional life events were again added to my plate of changes, one of which was not having any children to share with others. I attended a women's retreat a year later after Chad's death. Sitting at the breakfast table with the other ladies, the conversation around the table was about the women's children. Do not get me wrong. I want people to talk about their children and love to hear about each one. But that morning, the realization that I no longer had a child to share hit me hard. I quietly got up, returned to my room, and closed the door. Nothing that can fill this emptiness or the pain—your children are a very important part of your life, and now mine were gone. Nothing can replace them. This barrenness has forced me to enter other channels of my journey in an attempt to avoid some of the pain. This journey today continues to be in a hairpin curve, and God continues to hang onto me tightly through these days.

I was so blessed to have an exceptional son who had shown unusual compassion for me, who became a special friend, who walked with me on my journey, and who I was able to walk with on his journey. He is missed daily.

Linda and Chad at Biergarten restaurant at EPCOT (Walt Disney World)
December 2005

Chapter 15

᪥

I spent many hours on the web researching seizures after Chad's death. I had never heard of anyone dying while having a seizure and was stunned that this had taken Chad's life. But I kept seeing "sudden unexpected death in epilepsy" (SUDEP) in the reports and how common it was in young people who suffered with epileptic seizures.

In my research, I found many articles relating to head injuries and other symptoms that were part of Chad's history. I knew that he had suffered other symptoms, which always concerned him, and that he had discussed them with the doctor. Now I realized that they were due to his head injuries. Oh, how I wished I had known earlier and could have assisted in getting him help.

When Chad's autopsy report came in the mail in May, I opened it, expecting an answer within the twelve-page report. Everything came back negative and unremarkable concerning all his organs, including the brain. The mystery still existed, and I was so disappointed and frustrated that I still had no answers. In the back of my mind, I knew that Chad's death had to be related to the trauma of his head injury from the car wreck, but I needed to have an expert confirmation.

I went to the web looking for others who may have also died of seizure. In my search, I contacted the State of Oregon to see if they track the cause of death, which they do. I was given the web site where I found the statistics of those who had passed away from epileptic seizures. I was surprised with the results. During 1995-2004, there had been 171 deaths in Oregon contributed to epileptic seizures.

But I still could not put this mystery on the shelf and forget about it. I gathered the autopsy report and all of Chad's medical reports, including the reports from the wreck (since that was when he had his first major seizure that almost took his life), and sent them to the neurologist who was treating Chad to review.

Six weeks went by. Finally, the doctor called me into his office after he had reviewed and researched all the reports. He was extremely certain, without a doubt, that Chad's head injuries from the wreck were the cause of his present seizures. He explained that seizures beginning after twenty-eight years are very unusual, but it does occasionally occur after a serious trauma to the head. Typically, seizures would start from one to fifteen years after a head injury. But, he went on to explain, there was probably something that broke loose that had been injured during the wreck that was so minute that neither an MRI nor an autopsy were able to detect. He sent me home that afternoon with further information and his condolences. Finally, I had the truth about Chad's death; I now knew the "rest of the story."

My anger grew as I walked away from the doctor's office. I wanted to yell at that twenty-six-year-old man who drove intoxicated that night in November of 1977. Twenty-eight years later, he had taken yet another life. I did not lose five family members to a drunk driver, but six. I beat the steering wheel with my fists as I drove home.

PART SEVEN

"Promises are like the full moon: if they are not kept at once, they diminish day by day."

—German Proverb

Chapter 16

❧

The promise I made to Chad a few days after his grandmother's death to have a brick created for her at Walt Disney World Magic Kingdom kept coming to me. I needed to fulfill it, but this meant a trip to Disney World, and how I hated to tackle that trip without Chad. I thought several times that Chad would understand and forgive me if I did not fulfill the promise, but I knew how much it meant to him. I had to carry out my promise to him.

After much thought as to how to make this trip less painful, I chose to have six single friends join me who had not been there before. This would force me to approach Disney World in a different way. I would need to show them everything in the parks, which would, hopefully, lessen the pain of not having Chad and Mother there. Having friends by my side during this difficult trip was a blessing; I think only one or two really knew my true mission. God provided the course of action to ease the pain.

After researching on the web, I discovered with disappointment that Disney World had discontinued the bricks at the Magic Kingdom entrance. I could not carry out my promise! Now what? Since Chad and I had left our picture a few years earlier at EPCOT on the "Leave a Legacy" wall at the entrance, I realized that I could do the same for Mother and Chad. Leaving a small message would be even more special since EPCOT was their special park at Disney World. I knew that Chad would give his blessing too.

I hung my special plaque with the simple words around the corner from Chad's and my picture. Every time I entered EPCOT, I found the picture and plaque and gave each a greeting. On the final day of my trip, I lay a good-bye kiss on each. These small symbols at Disney World, along with all the other memories of my mother and Chad within the streets of magic, are special pleasures.

PART EIGHT

"Guess you better slow
that Mustang down."

—*Mustang Sally* by Sir Mack Rice

Chapter 17

❧

All that remains of the all-American Sundve family of the seventies are the house on the hill outside of Banks, Oregon, where I still reside today, and the 1966 baby blue Mustang. But both are just objects that can be replaced by another home or car; the members of the all-American family cannot be replaced.

The Mustang caused Gary and I to bump into each other for the first time and was a vital part of our family transportation for several years, including several trips, particularly Gary's and my honeymoon to Mt. Rushmore in South Dakota. "The Blue" brought both boys home from the hospital after their births and was filled with cookie and cracker crumbs in the backseat from their snacks. Tuffy, our dachshund, adored the back window and laid there for miles, wearing the paint away on the back window pane. He was looking for the next Diary Queen for his ice cream cone. "The Blue" truly was a special car. Hearing that magnificent 289-engine with the low rumbling pipes (that only older cars have) coming up the road was a delightful sound.

Ironically, though, "The Blue" had an encounter with a drunk driver and was almost destroyed, too. Chad and I had driven it to a friend's house in Hillsboro and parked in their driveway. About five minutes later, we heard squealing of tires and a loud crash very close to the house. A car had come around the corner, ran up and over the curb and into the yard, slammed into the rear end of the Mustang, and then raced down the street.

I was still able to drive the car home that night, since it was the rear end that got damaged, and the lights still worked on one side. But I was really shaken up over the incident. A few days later, while I was at the insurance inspection center to get an estimate of the damage to the Mustang, a man entered the office. He asked if I owned the Mustang outside and told me that he was the one who had hit it. I was surprised and shocked that we ran into each other since he did not stay at the accident scene but ran away. When he started laughing, and said he had been drinking when he hit the Mustang that night. Now here he was admitting to me what he had done.

I did not laugh about his intoxicated state, but instead told him and the whole office how drinking and driving had killed my family and that he had no business driving. It is beyond my comprehension why people think drinking and driving is a joke. It is a serious issue that can kill people. This incident with the Mustang just emphasized my fear: *Will this hideous crime ever stop?*

I am so grateful that no one was walking on the sidewalk and that we had not been in the car when he hit it. Only the car suffered damage. The insurance company wanted to total the car since the damage was equal to what the car was worth, but I wanted it repaired, if at all possible. "The Blue" was restored to its working state and driven several more miles before I slowed it down and retired it to the garage—where it sat until Chad rebuilt the engine and put his tender touches on the car. He drove it once in awhile with pride, knowing that he was driving the family's classic car that someday would be his.

Goldie, Linda, and Mandy in "The Blue" 2005

"Death is a challenge. It tells us not to waste time . . . It tells us to tell each other right now that we love each other."

—Leo Buscaglia

Conclusion

❧

No one is exempt from the injustice in this world, Christian or non-Christian. The experiences I have journeyed through would have been impossible without God carrying me through. Enduring those disasters alone would have been impossible. I must carry on with my journey, knowing that I will never be alone. God will forever be by my side.

My journey is one that I would never wish upon anyone. I truly do not understand it myself. Why did I have to take this journey? A drunk driver steered my life in another direction, and I am baffled as to how I have endured up to this point. I am still human and often desire to have different experiences in my life. I would love to see both of my sons as adults, maybe have daughters-in-law and even grandchildren, hearing their voices, and celebrating birthdays and holidays together. Mother's Day is the worst holiday to endure. It was painful without Kirk, but after Chad's death, the pain when I hear the advertisements and when I attend church that day is now utterly unbearable. And I would love to have had Gary to grow old with. But these desires and dreams were destroyed by someone who was thinking only of himself.

My desire as you have read about my experiences caused by a drunk driver, which I realize have not been pleasant, is that you understand that everyday more people are facing the same type of tragedy because people think that they can drive while being intoxicated. These people would never harm or kill anyone in their own mind, but think that it would only happen to someone else.

After Chad's death, I had to step down from public speaking. Relating the detail of the wreck over the last three decades was extremely painful before his death; adding his "rest of the story" was too heavy and disturbing. Sharing with others the message of how my family was killed is still very important to me. Hopefully, it will save other lives from being mangled and destroyed by an intoxicated driver. The Sundve's story must not stop! After the last page is read in this book, I hope that each reader will continue to fight this ugly crime by supporting tougher laws, sharing the Sundve story as a living example, and not allowing others to endure a lifetime of suffering as I have. If each person can save one life, the numbers can be decreased from fifteen thousand to zero deaths per year from alcohol-related wrecks in the United States.

The words that God spoke to Israel are the same words I rest on today: "The Lord appeared . . . I have loved you with an everlasting love; therefore I have continued my faithfulness to you. Again I will build you, and you shall be built" (Jeremiah 31:3-4).

I treasure the precious memories of my family. What God has done for me through my catastrophes, nourishing and restoring me, is beyond words. I will continue to look to Him as that beacon of hope that will always shine before me as I continue on this life's journey. Yes, life's journey must go on for me.

Acknowledgments

❧

To my dear friend, Brenda Kephart, for reading, editing, and sharing points of improvements to the manuscript, knowing that this was not an easy task, as it brought up hurtful memories for her to read and reminisce. Brenda and I have been friends since elementary school and lived in the same neighborhood and attended the same church while growing up. We spent hours together as teens riding around in her Chevrolet in Nampa and picked cherries together in the summer months. Most of all, I cherish our being able to share those teen's dreams together and being the maid of honor in each other's wedding. Her friendship is priceless.

After her marriage to Dan, our friendship continued to grow. More friends were added to the circle with Gary and eventually with Paul, Gary's brother. Paul lived with Gary and me for almost two years while he was attending college in Nampa. The five of us walked through countless days together that created endless memories: spending Saturday nights at the auto races during the summer months; having pizza at our favorite parlor in Boise every Sunday night after church; and more sharing of Sundve stories that generated an abundance of laughter. The day came when moving separated the five of us: Dan and Brenda to Washington, Paul back to Minnesota, and Gary and I to Oregon. Being separated physically did not endanger our friendships. We continued to mature together in our separate lives with new challenges and goals—the bond of friendship never broke. We shared the special events in each of our lives: Paul's marriage to Mary, the births of our children, and new careers. The hardest event was when Brenda was pulled out of choir on a Sunday morning in November and told that her friends were in a tragic wreck and that two of those friends were dead and another was hanging on to life.

Now, with just the three of us, Dan's and Brenda's friendship have become more important in my life. The many trips they made to be with me to give their support—even asking me if they needed to move closer—that is true friendship.

Brenda's telephone calls were always so concerned. She would ask, "How are you doing?" Once I answered with the general "Okay," she would reply, "Now, how are you *really* doing?" That three letter word, "now", assured me that she knew things were not okay and wanted to identify what was hurting me and listened. Thanks to Brenda and Dan for their enduring love and friendship.

To my sister, Peggy Litty, and her family, Roger, Barbara, Harry, Bruce, and Pam, for their bountiful support in each happening that I endured, whether a celebration of joy or unbelievable sadness. They were always by my side with their tenderness. Thank you, Peggy, for furnishing the picture of the car wreck for this book. She had told both Chad and me to let her know if we wanted to view it. Chad declined. I never wanted to view that wrecked car, as I was inside that crumbled, mangled mess. Knowing where everyone was located was too overwhelming for me. Gary had acquired that car in Oregon for his dad and mom, and we drove it back to Minnesota the year before with the two boys (Kirk's first car trip at two months old).

People often asked to see a picture of the wrecked car when I spoke, but I would only relate that I could not bear to view it yet. But I felt strongly that it should be included in this book. So, when I received the pictures in the mail from Peggy, God stood near, enabling me to observe it for the first time after thirty-three years. I am grateful that you kept and sent the picture, Peggy. Words cannot express the appreciation I have for you and your family for giving me endless hours of support. You were always there. To have you as my sister is a wonderful privilege, and I am proud to be your "sissy."

To Brent and Bryce Sundve and Cliff Nicholson for your inquiring spirit regarding the wreck and my speaking experiences when you where at my home at the time of Chad's memorial. The discussions stirred me to write additional information of my knowledge of the wreck to leave with you and your sister, Paula. Even though the incident that damaged and changed our lives is not pleasant to recall, it is vital part of our family history. Your mother, Mary, could write another book about what the intoxicated twenty-six-old man killed in your lives. Others could add more. This wreck had a ripple effect that has never stopped. Thank you, Brent, Bryce, and Cliff for jolting my spirit that day, even though the book only represents the sadness the family dealt with and not the true happiness of the Sundve family that I was able to enjoy for ten years. Mary, Brent, Bryce, Paula, and Cliff, you are very special to me, and I am glad that we are a family.

To Joleen Middleton, my dear Christian friend, who suggested I write a book about my journey. You have constantly stood by me not only in my darkest days after the wreck and Chad's death through prayers, visits, cards, telephone calls, and listening to my pain, but supporting me in so many other areas of my life. After your husband Don's death of a brain tumor (I still can hear Gary and Don laugh together), we developed a common thread, and our friendship has grown deeper, and new memories through the single's ministry, travels, and other events have been developed and valued. Your friendship is treasured.

About the Author

Linda Sundve graduated from Portland State University in 1991 with a Bachelor of Science in Economics. She was employed for eighteen years at Intel Corporation in both the accounting and finance departments. She retired in the spring of 2010.

The fight against drunk driving has been her focal point of concern. In 1980, she began volunteering for MADD in numerous positions, including serving on the board and engaging in speaking assignments at local schools and community meetings. She served twenty years as a panel member for the Victim Impact Panel program for both Washington and Columbia Counties in Oregon. She also did short commercials for a local television station during the mid-nineties during the Christmas and New Year's season. Linda also did a short blurb of the wreck and the losses in her life on the television program *Live with Regis and Kathie Lee* in the late nineties.

Linda may be reached via email: journey4568@earthlink.net